Praise for Willem Kuipers'
Enjoying the Gift of Being Uncommon:

In his book, *Enjoying the Gift of Being Uncommon*, Kuipers has ably addressed the dual difficulties of helping gifted adults acknowledge and celebrate their unique abilities. With clarity and gentleness, Kuipers opens doors to understanding with valuable specificity based on years of experience. This book belongs in the hands of all gifted adults as well as those who are close to them.
    Ellen D. Fiedler, Ph.D.
    Professor Emerita, Northeastern Illinois University, Chicago, IL, USA

It is unfortunately true that many bright, highly able, conscientious, and creative people feel out-of-sync with friends, neighbors, and fellow workers. They worry that there is something wrong with them and work hard to fit in, hiding their secret weirdness. This well-written and practical book provides good, positive feedback for such people. It outlines a process of recognition, exploration, and wise application of self-knowledge for success in the world and offers useful tools. Read and learn about practical ways to be most fully oneself.
    Betty Maxwell
    Director, Visual-Spatial Resource, Denver, CO, USA.

Many high ability people are uncomfortable with the label 'gifted' - but rejecting the label can also separate us from understanding and realizing our uncommon abilities. This book provides deep value by creating a new lens on being exceptional, with concepts for exploring and celebrating what it means to be unusually intense, complex and driven.
    Douglas Eby
    www.HighAbility.org, www.TalentDevelop.com.

Kuipers integrates a broad range of knowledge into a specific, cohesive, and concrete model that deftly circumvents the elitist connotation of the word gifted and replaces it with Xi, a more extensive and acceptable perspective. This comprehensive guide not only offers an opportunity for readers to discover, track, and actualize their potential but also provides a practical framework through which to filter their increasing self awareness.
Enjoying the Gift of Being Uncommon is for those individuals, across the lifespan, who hold a commitment to empathic understanding, authentic identity, and relational ethics toward a higher good.
    Janneke Frank, Ph.D.
    Principal Consultant, Frank Gifted Endeavours, Calgary, Canada,
    Coordinator, Gifted Education Certificate Program, University of Calgary.

Enjoying the Gift of Being Uncommon

Extra Intelligent,
Intense,
and Effective

Willem Kuipers

First USA edition, spring 2011.
Copyright © 2010, 2011 by Willem Kuipers
All rights reserved.
Interior design: Willem Kuipers and Paul Rüpp
Cover design: Paul Rüpp

ISBN-13: 978-1461185567
ISBN-10: 1461185564

Published by Kuipers & Van Kempen, Voorburg, the Netherlands.

Originally published with full colour illustrations in the Netherlands by Free Musketeers, Zoetermeer, 2010.
For the USA edition the full colour illustrations were converted to black-and-white ones, and a few typographical errors were corrected.

No part of this publication may be reproduced in any manner whatsoever without the prior written permission of the author, except for the inclusion of brief quotations in articles or reviews.

Contents

Foreword by Linda Silverman   ix

Preface   xiii

Introduction   1
    What is an extra intelligent person (XIP)?   1
    What is an Effective XIP?   4
    Why focus on enjoying this gift of being uncommon?   5
    How to Enjoy the Gift of Being Uncommon   7
    The impact of experiential knowledge   8
    The layout of this book   9

PART ONE   THE FIRST PRACTICE: ACKNOWLEDGING XI   11

Chapter 1   *Characteristics of Being Uncommon*   *13*
    The defining characteristics of an XIP   13
    Profile of an XIP: extra intense, complex and driven   15
    Xi and Giftedness   20
    Is it a Gift to be Uncommon?   25
    Superhuman or extra intelligent?   29
    A confusing variety of differences   31
    Possible scenarios for acknowledgement   33

Chapter 2   *The Complexity of Being Uncommon*   *39*
    Concerns about being different   39
    Who does not want to be an XIP?   41
    Recognition through vexation and reproaches   46

Chapter 3   *The Challenge of Acknowledgement*   *49*
    The asset behind the nuisance   49
    The underlying challenge of diversity management   51
    The possibilities of Ximension   54
    Good reasons to acknowledge Xi and XIPs   57

PART TWO   THE SECOND PRACTICE: EXPLORING XI   59

Chapter 4   Discovering Xidentity   61
    Multiple intelligences   65
    Imaginal thinking/verbal thinking   67
    Temperament   73
    Extravert/introvert   75
    Xinasty   77
    Extra empathy / task-orientation   79
    Extra receptivity   82
    Male/female archetypes   88
    The degree of Xi   92

PART THREE   THE THIRD PRACTICE: APPLYING XI   97

Chapter 5   The Diversity of Applying Xi   99
    Charting a course for the third Practice   99
    The diversity of excellence and leadership   102
    Superstars, strivers, independents   104

Chapter 6   Applying Xi amid the Norm   107
    Autonomy and rapport, interdependence   107
    Gift reciprocity versus market economy   112
    Performance and the personal challenge for mastery   117
    Is it excellence or deviance?   120
    The need for personal leadership   121

Chapter 7   Tools to Support the Process   123
    Mindset: Phrase compliments carefully   124
    Embodied Cognition (EC)   128
    Mirror Neurons (MNs)   131
    A map of stagnation and flowing expression   134

Chapter 8   Living happily ever after as an XIP   141
    Is it safe to accept being an XIP?   141
    The effective XIP, a work in progress   144

Appendix 1: A case of applying Xi — *147*

    The body and the mind, a brief intro on Chakras — 148
    Taking mind and body to a labyrinth — 153
    The Dynamics of expression — 156
    The path of flowing expression and of possible stagnation — 159

Appendix 2: Personal reflections on Xi — *167*

References — *169*

Websites — *172*

Index — *173*

Photographs, paintings, and figures in the book — *177*

The Ximension Foundation — *179*

Kuipers & Van Kempen — *180*

Figures

Figure 1: The realm of possible expression	21
Figure 2: Totally up to expectations	22
Figure 3: Two forms of underperformance	22
Figure 4: The same or quite different?	32
Figure 5: The Model of Xidentity	63
Figure 6: The diverging process of imaginal thinking	70
Figure 7: The converging process of verbal thinking	71
Figure 8: Overview of temperament characteristics	74
Figure 9: Superstars, exceeding expectations	104
Figure 10: Strivers, married to their work	105
Figure 11: Independents, not fitting in	106
Figure 12: Super pioneers: Changing expectations	116
Figure 13: Performance orientation may influence autonomy	118
Figure 14: Mastery, unexpected forms of proficiency	120
Figure 15: The labyrinth of stagnation	138
Figure 16: The labyrinth of flowing expression	139
Figure 17: The location of the seven chakras on the body	151
Figure 18: Classical labyrinth: pattern, path and its combination	155

Tables

Table 1: Top Ten criticisms and their implied sense of guilt	47
Table 2: Ten criticisms and their unseen special asset	50
Table 3: Female and male archetypes	89
Table 4: Labyrinth circuit, theme and colour	154

Foreword

The vast majority of gifted adults are never identified. Even those who were tested as children and placed in gifted programs often believe that their giftedness disappeared by the time they reached adulthood. It does not seem to matter how much success a person achieves—hardly anyone is comfortable saying, "I'm gifted."

That is why this book, *Enjoying the Gift of Being Uncommon*, is such a major breakthrough. Willem Kuipers bypasses the problem by coining a much more palatable term: eXtra intelligent (Xi). And, if someone has a knee-jerk reaction to that idea, Xi can also stand for eXtra intense. More people are aware of and admit to their intensity than to their uncommon intelligence. Parents note the intensity of their young child before they realize that their child is developing at a faster rate. High intensity is a close cousin to high intelligence.

Kuipers gently guides the reader and his clients through a process of self-recognition. He and his partner, Annelien van Kempen, have offered career counseling and identity development for eXtra intelligent adults for ten years. They know how painful it can be to feel so different from others and not understand why. They help their clients transform disconcerting qualities into positive resources that can be assets in the work world.

Enjoying the Gift of Being Uncommon describes three "Practices": acknowledging Xi, exploring Xi and applying Xi. The first step, acknowledging Xi, can be the most difficult. It requires a total re-definition of the Self. The process is facilitated when others recognize and support a person's uncommon intelligence.
There are five defining characteristics of eXtra intelligent/eXtra intense people (XIPs):

- *Intellectually able*
- *Incurably inquisitive*
- *Needs autonomy*
- *Excessive zeal in pursuit of interests*
- *Contrast between emotional and intellectual self-confidence*

It is not necessary for someone to identify with all five. Those who recognize themselves in at least three of the character traits may consider themselves XIPs. Self-recognition of one's uncommon constellation of abilities and personality traits is a powerful tool for self-development. It is transformative to discover that there are others who share the same characteristics, and that these are positive, rather than negative. Recognizing these traits in others and discussing Xi with them can be life-changing.

This expanded view of giftedness demonstrates the vast diversity of the population of XIPs. There are numerous ways of being intellectually able and an infinite number of pursuits that can captivate one's zeal. Therefore, no two XIPs are alike. However, they do share some basic characteristics, such as intensity, complexity, curiosity, drive and the need for autonomy. When these traits are mobilized, XIPs lead happy, productive lives, enhance corporate effectiveness, and may even change the world through their innovations. However, when these same traits are repressed, everyone suffers.

One of my favorite sections is the table of common reproaches that XIPs hear, and the delightful reframing of these as assets. For example, the criticism, "Can't you just keep one career direction?" can be translated into the unseen special asset of the "Ability to transcend borders among various disciplines."

Kuipers provides tips for corporations to effectively manage their most talented employees. He suggests that it can be very profitable for organizations to stimulate interaction between their XIPs, even when they do not work in the same department. "They will inspire and support each other to do their own job better…"

There is an extremely interesting discussion of "gift reciprocity versus market economy," based on the book, *The Gift*, by Lewis Hyde. XIPs may have difficulty charging sufficiently for their work, especially if they view their own abilities, products or insights as gifts that need to be shared with others. Society appears to be based on a market economy set up for the trading of commodities. Commodities are possessions. "In a gift society the highest esteem is for the person who gives the most. In a market economy, the highest esteem is for the person who takes the most."

This situation poses serious ethical and economic dilemmas for most gifted adults.

Enjoying the Gift of Being Uncommon is an important work that should be read by all who have ever wondered if they might be uncommonly intelligent, by all who live with and work with XIPs, by all parents of gifted children, by all corporations seeking to attract and keep highly competent employees, by all those who feel out-of-sync with society, and by all those who seek guidance in actualizing their potential. This book provides a blueprint for appreciating and mobilizing one's gifts to accomplish one's goals.

Linda Kreger Silverman, Ph.D.
Director
Gifted Development Center
Denver, Colorado, USA

Preface

E̲x̲tra I̲ntelligent P̲eople, XIPs for short, are a colourful lot: they can be brilliant, exasperating, full of ideas, dramatic, galvanizing or depressing, hilarious, persistently destructive, aloof or overwhelmingly helpful, and show many of these aspects even simultaneously. The list can be much longer but the shared aspects are "intense," "uncommon" and "diverse." My partner, Annelien van Kempen, and I were drawn into dealing with those XIPs through our own experiences:
- Our young daughter was labelled "gifted";
- We discovered – to our surprise – that we were "of the same kind" but still quite different in our expression of this quality;
- The clients of our coaching and counselling practice *Kuipers & Van Kempen* seemed to be highly intelligent when discreetly questioned, but would not consider themselves gifted at all.

Over the past ten years, we devoted our time to the exploration of how uncommon intelligence "works" in the private and professional lives of adults. We soon coined the concept of *e̲xtra i̲ntelligence*, or *Xi* for short, and connected it to five character traits that could be easily detected, either by the persons themselves, or by their environment. It proved practical to introduce the acronym *XIP* for *extra intelligent person* and *XIPs* for the plural *extra intelligent people*.

Our main goal was to combine and apply various scientific knowledge about uncommonly intelligent people, to help our clients to develop their own "manual." An important aspect was the revelation that many items in the manual were not about the extent of their cognitive intelligence, but about other facets of their personality, that proved to be uncommon or – in our terminology – "extra" too. Those facets were particularly relevant in their search for a more satisfying career or private life.

In fact, we gradually realized that we needed to develop our own applications of various theories on facets of personality, to address the specific qualities and needs of XIPs: They can show various qualities or extreme behaviours practically simultaneously, or can be extreme in a specific aspect. In short, XIPs are complex beings and need that complexity properly addressed to understand themselves fully and to use their wealth of qualities in a practical and effective way.

We thought it intriguing that effectiveness is seldom or never brought into connection with uncommon intelligence, let alone with the people who are gifted with it. Would that be one of the reasons why many of those adults so seldom are consciously and actively engaged in bringing their uncommon quality to full fruition? Would they just not know *how to do it*? Could it be that their environment is clueless too, when those various extraordinary talents do not thrive of their own accord?

That was the moment I decided to focus on writing about effectiveness of XIPs for the sake of XIPs and of their environment. I categorized our experience with the coaching of XIPs and our theoretical knowledge into three *Practices* that XIPs and their environment can relate to. We have worked with this approach for some time now, and it has proven to be a practical and effective tool in our communications on Xi and XIPs.

So here it is: This is a concise body of knowledge, based on pertinent literature and on ten years of extensive experience of coaching XIPs by Annelien and me. It is meant to be of value to both XIPs and their environment, in their professional and their private life. Please enjoy and take your own pick.

A book like this could not have been written without the help of many people. I want to thank them with all my heart:
Our dear friends and colleagues Mechel Ensing-Wijn, Amanda Bouman and Karien Boosten, who have been a generous source of inspiration. Paul Rüpp and Mariska Mallee, professional artists for much advice on aesthetics, mastery and more. Our friends and colleagues who were willing to read the manuscript and provide us with valuable comments, Frank Cornelissen, Geert Ensing, Peter Hoeben, Ardy Kuipers, Erik van de Linde, Betty Maxwell. Kumar Jamdagni and Grant Price who improved my expression in English. A special *thank you* to Linda Silverman who generously offered to write a foreword and gave editing advice.
Our clients for their trust, enthusiasm and perseverance.
Our daughter Georgina Kuipers, our muse for more than 18 years now, who prompted our interest in the subject and allowed us to discuss with and be inspired by many of her friends. And firstly and lastly my true partner in business and life, Annelien van Kempen.

Introduction

This book is about people that are in a specific way uncommon.
I will describe them, tell stories about them and share theories and experiences of living and effectively working with them.
What kind of uncommon people do I refer to? It is practical to use a name that in a way identifies them, and relates to their uncommonness as objectively as possible.

This book is about *eXtra Intelligent People*, or *XIPs* for short, and introduces three *Practices* that will help XIPs to enjoy their uncommon qualities through using them effectively. These Practices are anchor points for the self-management of XIPs, but also very practical for their environment to effectively manage, support and enjoy their XIPs.

There are various reasons why being uncommon is usually not asked for by XIPs. Viewing it as a *gift* clarifies some of those reasons, and helps to manage the consequences when these are somehow perceived as a predicament. The title is also a verbal link between the topic of this book and *giftedness* and those who are considered *gifted*: They can easily be characterized as XIPs, and the three Practices are fully applicable and useful to them as well.

Before I can elaborate on these Practices in the three Parts of this book, I need to set the stage: Explain my use of the concept of *extra intelligent people* and of *effectiveness*; give a short outline of the three Practices and their purpose; and illustrate our zeal in effectively combining action and reflection. Additionally there are some practical issues to address about the setup of the book itself.

WHAT IS AN EXTRA INTELLIGENT PERSON (XIP)?

From literature, statistics and experience it is clear that a small proportion of the population has an uncommonly high intelligence. This intelligence, broadly defined, can manifest itself in various forms including: theoretical or practical orientation, human interaction, music or sports orientation.
The shared characteristic is the uncommon level of this particular manifesta-

tion of intelligence, and the rarity – sometimes combined with peculiarity – of its existence. From statistics we know this applies to about 2% of the population, about one person in every fifty people.

In 2001 we[1] coined the concept of *extra intelligence* or *Xi* for short to indicate this uncommon level of intelligence. It is the *extra dose* of something that everyone basically has, which makes it notable and relevant for extra attention. More formally stated:

> *Extra intelligence indicates a subjectively verified, uncommonly high level of one or more kinds of intelligence.*

It is mostly used in the adjective form: Someone is extra intelligent, or someone is Xi. We call the owner of Xi an *extra intelligent person* or *XIP*, in the plural *extra intelligent people* or *XIPs*.

How can one recognize an XIP?

An XIP has three or more of the following five character traits:

1 Intellectually able
2 Incurably inquisitive
3 Needs autonomy
4 Excessive zeal in pursuit of interests
5 Contrast between emotional and intellectual self-confidence.

Traditionally, intelligence is measured by experts.
For instance, psychologists determine through IQ tests whether the qualification *gifted* is basically justified. Some experts maintain that an individual cannot be called gifted if that person does not deliver proper results at school, at university or at work.

Xi, on the other hand, can be identified by the very persons themselves or by someone in their environment. Furthermore, the boundaries of intelligence are broadened into *multiple intelligences* as introduced by Howard Gardner (1999). Therefore Xi can apply to verbal linguistic or mathematical logical

---

[1] "We" refers to Annelien van Kempen, my partner in business and life, and myself.

intelligence, but also to musical, interpersonal, bodily-kinaesthetic or visual-spatial intelligence, or any combination of those.

Please note that some of these intelligences are traditionally called talents, and that many people may not consider an owner of them as intellectually adept. As this is only one of the five character traits of an XIP, if three other traits are essentially identifiable, the hypothesis that this is an XIP may still be very valid. It is true, even if the implication of being an extra *intelligent* person seems awkward. This is elaborated on in chapter one.

So what if you recognize yourself and/or others as an XIP? Does that make you arrogant or rather opinionated?

The aim of the definition / description of an XIP is to offer a hypothesis based on an important personal characteristic. This hypothesis can be explored, validated and put to use as deemed appropriate to increase personal effectiveness and well-being.

It is meant to empower XIPs and to make them consciously aware that, although the phrase "extra intelligent" is part of their description, there is more to their nature than intelligence.

It is also meant to offer the social environment of XIPs, at their workplace or in their private life, a practical tool to become more easily aware of the *extra* qualities of XIPs, both in their positive and in their possibly negative aspects. This awareness and knowledge can be fruitful to XIPs and non-XIPs alike.

We firmly believe that:
- XIPs have the full authority to recognize and acknowledge their extra intelligence;
- They can only discern, experience and manage their uncommon qualities through the proper use of their own senses (including listening to others at times);
- They can flourish and enjoy their excellence more easily when they have adequate knowledge about their special condition.
- The social environment of XIPs will derive more benefits from XIPs when they have adequate knowledge about their special condition.
- The interaction among XIPs has a special quality to it. It speeds up, and becomes easily intense and very satisfying: We defined *Ximension* to be the extra dimension where being Xi goes without saying.

WHAT IS AN EFFECTIVE XIP?

Generally speaking, the word *effective* indicates the ability to produce a definite and desired effect or result.
American author Stephen Covey's notion of effectiveness[2] not only focuses in on the result itself, but also on the person desiring a result. He defines effectiveness as the balance between production of desired results and production capability (Covey, 2004).

> *"The essence of effectiveness is achieving the results you want in a way that enables you to get even more of these results in the future."* (p. 242)

It seemed to me that this approach of "sustainable production" is rare in the field of uncommon intelligent people.
There is a strong emphasis on the importance of proper schooling for gifted children, but little to no attention to the need for proper maintenance of giftedness for adults. If those adults do not produce as expected or become unable to do so, they may get rated as not gifted, after all.

In our work in Kuipers & Van Kempen with XIPs over the last ten years, we have been given sufficient proof by all our clients that maintenance and sustainability of their production capability is a very relevant and rewarding theme, and that it reframes, or greatly enhances their production.

Effectiveness does not always come by itself: It is the result of choosing wisely, which sometimes needs reflection and deliberation. But what would be the issues to consider? Why would those various extraordinary talents not automatically thrive and be productive? Why would a productive XIP after a couple of years get sidelined by a burnout? What could their environment do about it, especially as they are quite often well aware that something is going wrong with this XIP?
So we set out to connect effectiveness and uncommonly high intelligence in a way to be especially recognizable and applicable for XIPs and for their environments. In that process, we realized that we had been working with clients and developing workshops and instruments exactly in that line of

---

[2] As first introduced in: Covey, S.R. (1989). *The seven habits of highly effective people.*

thought. The conceptual framework of an *Effective XIP* fitted surprisingly well with our experiences, especially those acquired over the last five years. The pieces of the puzzle fell into place, and suddenly the *Three Practices of an Effective XIP* stood out very clearly and almost as a matter of course.

As a starter, the tentative definition of Effective XIPs is:

> *Effective Extra Intelligent People achieve the results that they aim to achieve, while optimally applying their extra intelligence, and consciously ensuring that their effort and its setting sustain their personal development and well-being in a balanced way.*

WHY FOCUS ON ENJOYING THIS GIFT OF BEING UNCOMMON?

One of the striking and disconcerting features of discussions about uncommonly high intelligence is the frequent mentioning of disappointment and rejection:

- Disappointment about unused talents and lack of drive or results on one hand and feelings of being rejected, underestimated, thwarted or denied on the other hand.
- Accusations against society not being able or willing to give their very talented citizens their due places to participate and contribute what they are worth.
- Accusations in return that they do not perform as might or should be expected and that they should back down as long as their performance has not improved.

It definitely takes conscious effort not to keep resonating to this resentment and to extensive lamentations about *the gifted adult condition* that are not very different compared to ten, twenty or more years ago. After all, many XIPs do carry old and fresh wounds caused by experiencing disappointment and rejection.

The central issue is that being uncommon may lead to uncommon challenges in finding one's way in life and work. The tricky part is not being aware that these challenges exist and as a result becoming overwhelmed by one or

more of them. That is where the need comes in for properly managing this uncommonness as part of actively enjoying it.
What are those challenges that I refer to?

The first challenge has to do with being uncommon as such. This is for some people not an issue, and for others a long struggle with their memories. It is a very relevant step to realize that some of one's personal qualities are quantitatively and/or qualitatively and positively very unusual. The next step is to consciously accept these qualities to their full extent amidst other people.

The second challenge has to do with the discovery of personal strengths and weaknesses. It is a challenge because they are uncommon too and may not be readily seen or accepted by one's environment and by oneself. We coined the phrase *Xidentity* to bring together a number of personal characteristics, which properly address the Xi-aspects and its variations among different XIPs. An *exploration* of one's Xidentity is a key-factor in finding the right subject for effective action.

The third challenge is about finding one's own way in the process of striving for actual excellent results while using one's uncommon qualities and respecting one's uncommon needs. It is a twofold challenge because there is often a fulfilment of expectations at stake and because excellence has a natural mismatch with normalcy. This may possibly lead to confusion and disappointment about the difference between an *excellent performance* as experienced by the environment, and the *process of expressing excellence or mastery*. Excellent performance is not a matter of course for many XIPs and they face specific challenges, given their XIP-ness. Sometimes not meeting others' expectations is the only way to strive for discovering something truly new. But it can be a very lonesome road to travel on, especially when the road is long and winding.

These three challenges illustrate that there is most often some work to do for XIPs who want to enjoy their being uncommon in an effective way.
In the next section I will introduce three tools to support that process.

How to Enjoy the Gift of Being Uncommon

The issue of *Enjoying the gift of being uncommon; extra intelligent, intense, and effective,* centres around three focal points. Because we have come to the conclusion that these issues are in fact *actual applications of a method with a need for repeated exercise to maintain proficiency* we have named them *Practices.*

These are the three Practices, as phrased for XIPs themselves:

1 *Acknowledge Xi*: Recognize and accept being an XIP with all its aspects of being uncommon in some needs, possibilities, habits, and output. Discover other XIPs and value the special interaction with them in Ximension.
2 *Explore Xi*: Investigate how you are Xi, consider the various aspects of your Xidentity and embrace its strengths, weaknesses, opportunities and threats.
3 *Apply Xi*: Decide to apply that "extra-ness" of your extra intelligence to the world, become consciously aware of the process required to allow for your expression of mastery and excellence, and go for it with all your passion and determination. Your performance will be worth your efforts. Do not forget to take time to enjoy this.

One might wonder: "Is that all there is to it? Only three Practices?"
Do not be misled, this is a mouthful, as will become clear in the following three parts of this book, each of them dedicated to one of the three Practices. The strength of this new approach lies in:

- Making clear *why* just being noted as "uncommonly intelligent" is not a helpful guarantee for excellent performance;
- Connecting the subject of effectiveness to the conciseness of just three Practices;
- Stimulating awareness that these Practices have to be practiced to help any XIP become an effective XIP;
- Addressing the whole XIP, not just his/her intelligence;
- Drawing attention to the enormous diversity that can be found in this tiny category of the population;

- Putting into words and analyzing the considerable emotional impact of being an XIP;
- Offering a framework for recognition and for support and facilitation of their effectiveness to the environment of XIPs including their work environment.

THE IMPACT OF EXPERIENTIAL KNOWLEDGE

Ten years ago we did not have a clear-cut plan on how to develop, use and communicate the body of knowledge we were acquiring on Xi. We were driven by our own questions, having encountered the subject of giftedness and wondering what to think of it and how to use it in a proper way. From the beginning we were also intrigued by how it affected us personally in our well-being, in the way we worked, in the expression of our uncommon zeal and in many other personal facets. During these ten years Annelien and I have experienced how we differed in our approach to these subjects:
She preferred to discover in action; I was the one to read, reflect and write. She developed workshops and training sessions like *Birds of a feather flock together* and *Training Mastery*; I developed counselling tools and concepts like *Xi, Xidentity, Ximension, Extra Empathy and Extra Task-orientation*. She found out that she wanted to meet clients in their work or private environment; I most often met them in our office at home. She built a relation network and together with them organized Round Table meetings, mini-conferences and the Ximension Foundation; I built various websites to make our acquired knowledge available. She brought the outside world in; I brought the inside world out. She tempted me into actions; I charmed her with my reflections. Of course we did many projects together, and, most importantly, we always reflected together on all of our actions concerning Xi, learning from it and enjoying our complementarity.

Around 2007 we discussed the effectiveness of our approach with Dr. Ariane Oberndorff-De Wilde, a company physician who had obtained her doctorate from the University of Maastricht in 2000. She had discovered that knowledge about Xi was very useful in her professional practice and was keen to research its effects more deeply. She offered to investigate the effectiveness of our Xi career counselling to obtain an objective view and to increase applicability for companies. Sixteen clients were selected and were asked for their

consent. Ariane made a qualitative analysis of their files and conducted semi-structured telephonic interviews, asking questions about their previous role at work, their current role and the influence of our coaching.
She concluded that clients experience various changes through Xi-coaching:

- They gain more insight, awareness and acceptance of their extra intelligent identity.
- They learn to embrace their own qualities and actively engage in making them visible to their environment.
- They increase their self-confidence and become less vulnerable in a changing environment; they feel better able to choose what is right and effective for them.
- They are better able to explain in due course their "own manual" to their work environment, preventing irritation or lack of understanding.
- They feel more autonomous and free to express their creativity at work.

She has presented with Dr. Noks Nauta at the 2009 conference of the Netherlands Society of Occupational Medicine on the "manual" of gifted employees.
Her research has confirmed to us that the best approach to increasing effectiveness of XIPs is offering action and reflection, both to the XIPs and to their environments. This works in two, mutually influencing ways:

- XIPs become more effective in their work and their personal lives;
- More experiential knowledge about Xi and XIPs becomes available and can be verified in practice by XIPs and their environment.

By publishing this book in English we intend to contribute to both goals: The knowledge that we have acquired and developed becomes available to a much wider audience and will be verified and practiced by more XIPs and their environment. Please enjoy the gift of being uncommon!

THE LAYOUT OF THIS BOOK

The main body of the book is dedicated to the three Practices. These three Practices *Acknowledging Xi*, *Exploring Xi*, and *Applying Xi*, can be found in the Parts I, II and III, respectively. Each Part consists of one or more Chapters, and the Chapters have Sections.

Appendix 1 elaborates on the underlying theory and concepts of the *Maps of Stagnation and Flowing Expression* as introduced in chapter seven.
It is a characteristic example of the variety of topics, that XIPs naturally wish to address when applying their Xi, expressing themselves as they essentially are: complex, intense and driven.
Appendix 2 offers personal reflection on your own relation to the subject of Xi.

The list of References that were used for this book has been limited; the book is not meant to be a scientific treatise and as a consequence, not every statement is referenced. On the other hand I have added some relevant sources for my work to the list, without citing them explicitly in the text.
The English title of books is used, even when I have read them (firstly) in Dutch. A few Dutch books are included, as they have been an important source for my work.
The Index offers main references to the mentioned topics.

The book has been written by me, Willem Kuipers. I have chosen to use "I" and "me," when indicating my personal opinion or experience.
The body of knowledge, however, has been developed in our coaching practice in very intense cooperation with my partner Annelien van Kempen. That is why I use "we" and "our" to indicate our shared opinions and experience.

I use two types of italics for quotations and other illustrative remarks.

> *These are the kind of italics that I will use for quotations, illustrations or stories by others.*

> *These are the kind of italics that I will use to indicate illustrations and stories that refer directly to my personal experience and development issues.*

The stage has been set:
Onward to the first Practice; *Acknowledging extra intelligence.*

PART ONE

THE FIRST PRACTICE: ACKNOWLEDGING XI

Chapter 1 *Characteristics of Being Uncommon*

The first Practice to manage the gift and further effectiveness is about recognition and acceptance of extra intelligent people (XIPs) in all aspects of their being uncommon in some needs, possibilities, habits, and output. It is also about the discovery and appreciation of the special interaction among XIPs in *Ximension*.
Recognition can be fairly straightforward, based on identification with the various characteristics of Xi and of XIPs that are mentioned in the next sections of this first chapter.

But there is also a need for acceptance of this conclusion to make the acknowledgement effective, preferably both by the XIPs and by their environment. This process of only gradual acceptance of the conclusion is highly influenced by emotions: As long as they cannot accept the idea of being an XIP, they will strongly deny their recognition of the characteristics, or they will express doubts about their relevance, even if they grudgingly admit some possibility. Similarly, managers and co-workers of XIPs may have problems with recognition, because they are most vexed by their apparent unpredictable and reproachable behaviour. Chapter two discusses these complex processes.

Managing diversity is hard work and it sometimes takes courage to overcome the nuisance, and acknowledge the asset behind it. It may rightly be called a challenge to acknowledge the extra intelligence of XIPs and find the specific way to use it effectively. One of these ways is to consider the organization and support of Ximension. As I conclude in chapter three, there are good reasons to acknowledge Xi and XIPs, both for themselves and for their environment at the workplace and in their personal sphere.

THE DEFINING CHARACTERISTICS OF AN XIP

Extra intelligent people – XIPs – are people who can essentially identify with three or more of the following five character traits or can be identified by others as possessing these character traits:

1 *Intellectually able*: Grasps complicated issues relatively easily, able to take substantial leaps in the thinking process, has a low tolerance for stupidity, and may become careless when asked to do simple tasks.
2 *Incurably inquisitive*: Always curious about what lies beyond the horizon, fascinated as long as something is new, easily pursuing manifold interests. Has a low tolerance for boredom and may be slow in bringing to a conclusion a problem once it has been solved.
3 *Needs autonomy*: Can work on his/her own and prefers to schedule tasks independently. Will respond aversely to absolute power and formalities and react allergically to superiors or others who exercise tight control. Will utilize fight or flight when autonomy is threatened.
4 *Excessive zeal in pursuit of interests*: Can be inexhaustible and keyed-up as long as a problem is interesting and still unsolved but will drop it readily when the specific curiosity has been satisfied. Can invest too much energy in the wrong projects. Does not like others to perform according to low standards.
5 *Contrast between emotional and intellectual self-confidence*: Either can be relatively high, while the other is poorly established or even low.
Some know in their mind that they are right, but fear in their gut that they will not win the case. Others feel quite confident that they will manage to realize their intentions, but dread being tackled about their intellectual qualities.
This can easily lead to perfectionism, fear of failure, or escalating "know-it-all" tendencies, nagging and arrogance in an effort to mask the uncertainty. Some XIPs are vulnerable to senseless or blunt displays of power.

In Appendix 2 (p. 167) I have included a question sheet to mark your own measure of recognition of these characteristics and to specify your interest in the subject of Xi, for your personal record and reflection.

For all those who recognise themselves in essence in at least three of the five character traits mentioned, we believe that it is worth the effort to consider the validity of the hypothesis "I am an XIP" or alternatively, "I act like an XIP." The same applies to those who are recognized by others as such.
This can be done by exploring in more detail the possibility of having an uncommonly high intelligence in the *widest* sense. Although in theory this could lead to a situation in which people deceive themselves by imagining

something that is totally unrecognisable for others, this approach has, for almost ten years now, proven to be remarkably effective in practice.

Similarly, putting the threshold at the essential recognition of *three or more* out of five characteristics has proven to work fine. There are many XIPs who are not bothered by the fifth characteristic, and who initially do not consider one of the other four characteristics very applicable to themselves. Consider the case, however, that people would recognize themselves to some extent in three of the five characteristics, but find little added value in the connected body of knowledge about Xi. They may still consider it worth the effort to have investigated it, but one may safely assume that they will limit their efforts in relation to the perceived added value of pursuing the subject any further.

Extra intelligence is, after all, not always an exclusively positive qualification: Just as a sharp knife can cut impeccably thin slices but can also easily wound a person, it is not necessarily a blessing to be (like) an XIP. Just as with the knife, the essence is not so much *whether* it is so, but *how* to properly manage its operation.
In many cases, the recognition of Xi is hardly a rational issue: Due to all kinds of preconceptions about "people with uncommonly high intelligence," judgments about oneself or another may be negatively biased: "How could I be an XIP?!" or "How could she be an XIP?!" even while recognition of all five characteristics is very strong and not disputed. In chapter 2 we elaborate on emotional barriers to recognition and acceptance, both for XIPs and their environment. But firstly we offer more technical information on the characteristics and recognition of extra intelligence and XIPs.

PROFILE OF AN XIP: EXTRA INTENSE, COMPLEX AND DRIVEN

In her book, *The Gifted Adult,* American author Mary-Elaine Jacobsen (1999) introduces the term *Everyday Genius* to characterize gifted adults and describes their development and behaviour extensively.
We have found her description of *The Big Three Differences* (p. 253) very practical to convey a kind of summarized profile of XIPs.
Everyday Geniuses, hereafter referred to as XIPs, are different in three fundamental ways: quantitatively, qualitatively, and motivationally.

They lead more *intense* lives, think in more *complex* ways, and are more *driven* than normally endowed individuals.
The key is to turn these special characteristics to your advantage rather than to allow them to work against you.

Intensity

XIPs are quantitatively different; all systems are running at full throttle. They experience the world more intensely and respond in a corresponding manner. Their senses observe more nuances but are also more susceptible to becoming overloaded. They are able to concentrate in an extraordinarily focussed manner and have strong powers of empathy plus an inexhaustible energy for enterprise. They have a deep and exuberant sense of humour and ability to put things into perspective.
If they are not operating in strength mode, these qualities become distorted in an extremely active or passive form: XIPs can be depressive, workaholic, or know-it-all, becoming a ruthless debater, torturer or martyr, cynic, iceberg, or unguided missile to mention but a few possibilities.

Complexity

XIPs are qualitatively different; they can absorb, analyse, and synthesise information from a wide range of domains extremely rapidly and even simultaneously.
This is an extremely influential characteristic that results in multiple interests, a pervasive sense of self-consciousness, extraordinary intuitive powers, a huge memory for all kinds of things, and a capacity for original and complex trains of thought.
If this complexity is not managed properly, once again extreme effects will arise: obsession with one theme, or too little attention across too many themes, self-hate, fear of the irrational or escape into superstition, tunnel vision, manipulation, production of trivial facts, chaos without content, or analysis without conclusion.

Drive

XIPs are unusually driven individuals; they are structurally inquisitive, set the bar at a high level, and are self-starting, independent, and persistent.

They have an inner drive, even though they initially may be unaware of where this will lead. This makes them natural innovators and visionaries, idealists, and strong performers who are flexible, and adept at achieving their objectives.

Here, too, the key to success lies in finding appropriate resources. If this does not happen, stagnation will occur via fear of failure, or ultimate perfectionism. Alternatively, a good start will never be capitalised upon and concluded. Or the wheel will be re-invented. Some individuals allow themselves to be pushed just so they can resist. Others manage to discourage everyone through their endless nagging.

XIP: eXtra **Intense** *Person*

Intensity is quite often a very defining characteristic of XIPs, especially when used to describe their style of personal expression. It may even be a more apparent characteristic than being uncommonly intelligent. In fact, we have encountered many people who are in our opinion true to type XIPs, but who told us that they have great objections to the implication that they could be extra *intelligent,* as the term "extra intelligent person" suggests.

Formally, there is no problem, as the definition of XIP states that recognition of three out of five characteristics is sufficient reason to explore the subject further, and uncommon intelligence is only one of the five.

We decided that XIP could also be the acronym for eXtra *Intense* Person.

Practically speaking, those XIPs do have uncommon intelligences, but often not the "high IQ score" kind. They may recognize the fifth characteristic of Xi (*contrast between emotional and intellectual self-confidence*) in the specific form of: *emotionally stable, intellectually insecure* instead of the other way around. Often it seems to be combined with a strong preference for imaginal thinking (see chapter 4), which may have caused difficulties in mastering academic (strongly sequential verbal thinking) knowledge.

Given their recognition of three or more of the five characteristics of Xi, and as long as they feel that it is not appropriate to consider themselves extra *intelligent,* let them please call themselves an extra *intense* person and, just like all XIPs, find out what information about XIPs is relevant for their personal situation. That is, after all, what our intention with the concept of XIPs is about.

Hans shows his utter focus and intensity while playing on one of his bass guitars. It is an illustration of his excessive zeal in everything he undertakes. The quality of his instruments is very crucial to him due to his high sensitivity and musical abilities.

Annelien shows in this picture her vulnerable emotional self-confidence while most people in her environment know her as active and self-confident. Behind her are examples of her creativity in creating glass objects. She is persistently inquisitive about new ways to express herself.

Xi and Giftedness

The typical character traits of gifted people, as documented in numerous references, are fully applicable to XIPs.
Similarly, almost all gifted people will essentially identify with three or more of the five characteristics of an XIP.
However, the differing methods of determining whether someone is an XIP or a gifted person, and the terminology that is used, makes Xi and giftedness two different approaches to identify and describe uncommon intelligence. In a nutshell, all gifted people can be recognized as XIPs with the aid of the five characteristics of Xi, but not all XIPs will succeed in being designated as gifted through formal IQ testing.

There are three essential differences between Xi and giftedness.

1. Xi, "extra intelligence," is not linked to any formal testing procedure, while giftedness is formally linked to a sufficiently high score on a formally accredited IQ test that is taken under standardised conditions (with possibly achievement scores and checklists of characteristics also.)
   This is why, based on experience and acknowledgement, someone may call himself/herself extra intelligent, or be assigned that description by someone else. Giftedness, on the other hand, is usually confirmed only after formal research by an independent third party who is an authorised professional in that field.
2. Not all XIPs will achieve an extremely high (98th percentile) IQ score. Because IQ tests measure specific types of intelligences, people who are extraordinarily adept in other domains will score too low, while being still clearly recognisable as XIPs. Think of fields such as sport, music, architecture, art, theatre, but also, for example, of charismatic leadership. Additionally some XIPs will experience an emotional or practical (e.g., dyslexia) barrier while taking an IQ test, and will therefore score too low, or avoid being tested.
3. Giftedness refers literally to special talents provided at birth, something that arouses high expectations of special feats by the owner of these talents, at school and at work.
   Xi refers literally to a certain extra something, compared to standard availability or necessity; a kind of overdose without implicit expectations for high achievements.

There is more to write in connection to the third difference, given the title of this book, *Enjoying the Gift of Being Uncommon*. Can being extra intelligent also be considered as a gift provided at birth? What are the consequences of that viewpoint or mental experience?

I will return to that issue in the next section. But firstly I want to expand on the first difference.

A different perspective

The mentioned first difference can also be seen as a difference in perspective between giftedness and Xi: The notion of giftedness uses the perspective of an expert observer who assesses whether the observed person can be considered a valid member of a certain category. The notion of Xi invites to take the perspective of the XIPs themselves. It addresses the themes that are relevant from that perspective, like "what is it like to be an XIP."

It is like the difference between the making of a portrait or a self-portrait.

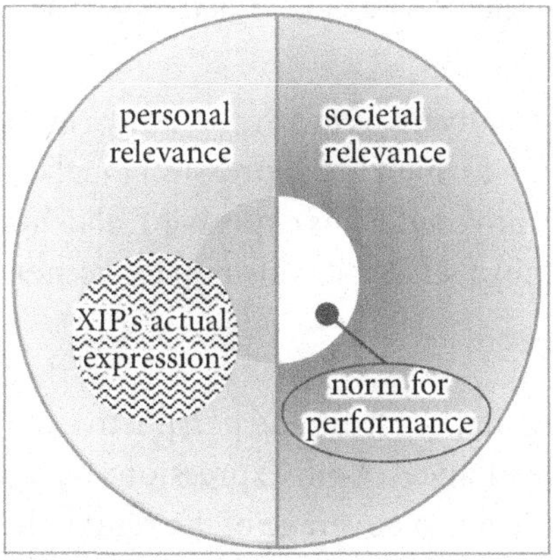

Figure 1: The realm of possible expression

In figure 1 this difference in perspective is illustrated through a basic graph, that I will also use in varying forms in part III.

The circle indicates the realm of possible expression of an XIP: It is the domain where the XIP can accomplish activities. The realm is divided in two halves. The right half is that part of the realm where activities have apparent societal relevance.

The white half-circle indicates the specific expectations of society with regard to the behaviour of someone that is considered gifted. The word "performance" refers to the process of carrying out or accomplishing an action and specifically to how successfully a duty or a promise is realized. The perspective of adult giftedness focuses most often on what happens in the right half of the realm.

The left half is that part of the realm where the activities mainly have a personal relevance for the XIP. They may bring on great personal satisfaction. The perspective of the XIP is the entire realm of his/her possible expression.

"Expression" refers to the process of making one's thoughts *and* feelings known, making them public. This can take various forms. Some of these forms may be more attractive to society while others are less attractive or not attractive at all.

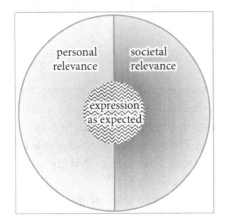

Figure 2: Totally up to expectations

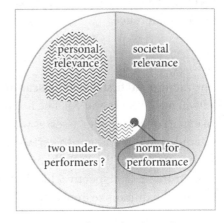

Figure 3: Two forms of underperformance

Figure 2 illustrates gifted behaviour that is totally up to the expected norm. This is shown through the compliance of the form of the expression to what was expected: The white half-circle is fully covered. This expression also has an aspect of personal relevance: The XIP may feel that it is also up to his/her own standards of expectation.

Figure 3 shows two variations of something that is – from the perspective of giftedness – most often named "underperformance". Both expressions have little societal relevance, shown through little or no coverage of the right half of the realm. Neither of the two forms matches the expected norm for performance at all.

From the perspective of Xi, however, these forms refer to two different situations. The small one may be considered as typical for stagnated expression: The form is relatively small and has little contrast. The large form may refer to a personal breakthrough or a very elaborate expression. It may be interpreted as a powerful indication of the extra intelligence of that person.

Although one can, too, observe XIPs and measure their performance, it is the intention of our approach to facilitate individuals to become aware of

their entire realm of possibilities for expression. That includes the half that has only personal relevance and may call for reflection on personal growth. Because XIPs are by definition uncommon, it helps them to become aware how their uncommonness relates to different perspectives on the value of personal expression and of performance as expected.
Additionally, by explicitly involving the XIPs themselves, other information about XIPs becomes available to society compared to the situation where experts and their observations are the main source and reference. XIPs can use their intrapersonal intelligence to be reflective practitioners on the subject of their own effectiveness.

XIPs reassured by their IQ score

At the beginning of this section I summarized the relation between XIPs and gifted people with regard to their IQ score.

> *In a nutshell, all gifted people can be recognized as XIPs with the aid of the five characteristics of Xi, but not all XIPs will succeed in being designated as gifted through formal IQ testing.*

Some of our clients have absolutely no desire to know their IQ score. Some of them would probably score well in the gifted range, of others I am not too sure due to their differing kinds of intelligence. But at times there are clients who explain to us how knowing their IQ score would help them to accept being an XIP more readily. Some of them have not finished their university studies or left school early. They want to understand how this could happen and are interested in their strengths and weaknesses. Others may feel that a high IQ score will help their environment to accept them being uncommonly intelligent, notwithstanding their curriculum vitae.
I may add that people who like working with numbers seem to understand information better when it is quantified. Having an IQ score of 150 is very well understood by them, while explaining that they are extremely intelligent does not have the same impact.

Our friend Karien Boosten is a licensed psychologist with a keen eye for observing test stress and with a lot of patience to accommodate clients to overcome their anxieties.

In the spring of 2010 – during a mini-conference on applying Xi – she presented her analysis of twelve of our clients that had come to her for IQ testing. These twelve varied in age (20-50) and education level (no university grades and far less, many retries). They shared experiences of getting the wrong jobs and had struggled to find out what would really suit their qualities. They had found out that they were somehow more intelligent than their environment due to their fast thinking and smart acting.
Some were frustrated by the lack of understanding of their plans and actions by their environment.

In her analysis she listed quite a number of ineffective work strategies and limiting beliefs that impeded the testing. She somehow had managed, however, to make them regain their confidence or their abilities and to test them according to the official rules. All twelve scored in the gifted range. In seven cases the verbal tests scored higher than the performal ones, in four cases it was the other way around.

She confirmed that the test score had been a major relief for the clients. We were aware of that, as many had told us their stories afterwards. The analysis also showed that these clients might not have obtained a similar score under harsher conditions like collective test sessions or impatient testers.
In chapter two I will explain the emotional complexity of recognition of extra intelligence in more detail.

A new Dutch definition of giftedness

In 2006 a group of about twenty Dutch experts on giftedness were invited by W. Wind and M. van Thiel to join efforts in creating a new definition of giftedness, using aspects of the Delphi method[3]. I participated as well.
My tentative English translation of this new definition is:

---

[3] This variation of the Delphi Method used rounds of questionnaires to a panel of experts to come to a consensus on the new definition. After each round the facilitator summarized anonymously the various opinions, which were used as context for the next round of questions. The results were presented at a congress and expounded on in a book (Kooijman-van Thiel ed., 2008).

A gifted person is a speedy and smart thinker, able to deal with complex issues. By disposition autonomous, inquisitive and driven.
A sensitive and emotional human being, living intensely.
He/she derives pleasure from creating.

This new Dutch definition approaches giftedness in a positive and more accessible way and shows many similarities with the characteristics of Xi.
The unresolved issue is whether it is "allowed" to use the definition in reverse order: If you recognize yourself in this new definition, does it follow that you are gifted?

I know that some members of the panel of experts will agree with this and some will definitely not. Probably this will also be the case for the general public.
Additionally, the definition opens with the *thinking* quality, referring to specific cognitive abilities. In our own experience, many XIPs are more focused on their *intense doing* than on their *smart thinking*, which they consider something for intellectual people or which they take for granted. Although they can be made aware that they do have a flash of *speedy and smart thinking* before they act, it is not something they readily identify with. The other mentioned qualities in the definition will be more easily recognizable for them.
Please note that we will use the word *giftedness* now and again in this book: Either due to references to relevant sources, or due to the partial overlap with the concept of Xi.

IS IT A GIFT TO BE UNCOMMON?

As was mentioned in the previous section, giftedness refers literally to special talents, somehow provided at birth. Extra intelligence refers literally to an uncommon overdose, compared to standard availability.
It is well known that the label *gifted* is generally not welcomed by the person in question, whether child or adult. This can be due to worries about possible stigmatization as a strange exception to normal, or about the implied expectation or felt obligation to be an outstanding performer.
Annelien and I have always considered it one of the benefits of the term of Extra Intelligence, that there are less implicit burdens connected to it.

And of course the other two differences – personal recognition instead of formal link to IQ score and the extension to all domains of multiple intelligences – added good reasons to coin the concept.

Recently, however, while studying more deeply these implicit burdens of being called gifted, we came to realize that there is an extra issue to address: *Does being Xi feel like a gift or like a commodity?*

> We both had read the book by American author Lewis Hyde: "The Gift. Creativity and the Artist in the Modern World" (2007) [4].
> Triggered by the leading title, we noticed that the book does not address the case of the so called intellectually gifted. Its partly anthropological explanation of gifts as a kind of circulating wealth and gift-exchange as a special kind of commerce, however, matches perfectly with themes we have encountered in our work. Additionally, many statements that Hyde makes about artists and their work can be easily transferred to XIPs and their expression. This is especially true when these XIPs are relatively independent and creative. Issues like performance as (not) expected, market value, and contribution to society are very similar indeed. This interpretation also offers remarkable insights about dominant societal views on giftedness and uncommon intelligence.

One's view on this issue of whether being Xi feels like a gift or like a commodity, influences one's choices in the management of this uncommonness. In this section I will address the characteristics of the XIPs who tend to choose the first option. The tension between the rules of gift-exchange versus market economy and its effects on different XIPs are explained as part of the third Practice, in chapter six. I will briefly cite and explain the concepts as put forward by Hyde in his book, and then add my own application of these concepts to extra intelligence and giftedness.

Driven to use and share their Gift

A gift is something we do not get by our own efforts: It is bestowed upon us. That makes it different from something we acquire through our own efforts,

---

[4] The cited book is actually the twenty-fifth anniversary edition and the author has added an inspiring afterword on the puzzle of how to support creative work in the present dominance of market economic thinking.

like commodities or possessions. Giving and gifts play an important role in our celebrations and generally in the affirmation of mutual relations.
At birthdays for instance, we celebrate the gift of having lived for another year, we offer gifts and hospitality to our dear ones and receive their gifts in return. Gifts have to be reciprocated to keep their essence of being a gift; that is maintaining the relation.

A talent is a gift: Although one needs to develop the talent through conscious effort, its initial appearance is a gift.
Inspiration and intuition are also a gift: Their appearance cannot be forced or adequately forecasted. Therefore, the *creation* of a true work of art comes partly as a gift to the artist, and many artists feel that way about their creations.
Hyde argues that looking at such a work of art conveys an awareness of that gift to the beholder. That makes it *art* instead of an everyday commodity: We are touched by it *gift-like*, in a way that has no direct relation with the price we paid for museum entry or even ownership.
Thus many artists feel grateful that talents and inspiration have been bestowed upon them. They feel the urge to share the results with their environment, and their gift is reciprocated through public attention, admiration, official prizes, and, to some extent, through money to account for their daily costs of living.
How does Hyde's description translate to XIPs and their *gift of being uncommon*?

There are XIPs who consider their uncommon intelligence somehow as a gift; they certainly did not ask for it at birth. Others may consider it an act of God, a weird trick of fate, a cosmic joke or a genetic inevitability. But in all cases there is most often a drive to do something special with it, a sense of mission, even when the mission itself is far from understood as yet.
Additionally, many XIPs are aware that they can have curious bursts of creativity. Their inspiration to be creative comes regularly, but still at unexpected moments, and its results can often amaze themselves and their environment.

It is our experience that many XIPs, when they recognize their being Xi, express an urge to use their *gifts* to improve the world, to provide help by solving very complicated social problems and the like. They do not necessarily expect to be paid abundantly but would like to get some credits in return. In other words, they experience a drive to continue the cycle of giving, and are definitely not focused on getting the highest price for their scarce commodity.

Although honourable as an intention, this attitude is not always practical. It leaves the XIP especially vulnerable when the offered gifts are criticized or refused by the intended recipients: implicitly or even explicitly, they make clear that they do not value the offered gift. Thereby they refuse (the continuation of) the relation with the XIP. As a result, the XIP may start to question the value of the gift, and decide to stop using it or deny having it, as it brings no good, after all. This can lead to stagnation of personal expression and development.
There are to my knowledge no standard recipes for the prevention of this kind of stagnation. Not taking the criticisms as personal reproaches helps, as will be illustrated further on. Being aware that the issue exists helps too, and that is one of the reasons to have mentioned it here and now. I will come back to that perspective in chapter six in the section on "Is it excellence or deviance?"

Fortunately, however, many XIPs thrive thanks to a stimulating environment, or a very independent mind which is hardly influenced by other people's opinions: Their characteristic *drive* and *intensity* come in handy there.

> I have a hypothesis that being very aware of one's extra intelligence and especially one's uncommon creative inspiration, almost entails considering this condition as something like a gift. Or the other way around, the less one considers one's Xi or creative inspiration to be something special, the easier it is to ask for and accept payments like one does for a commodity.
> I will come back to this hypothesis in chapter six in the section on Gift reciprocity.

But let us now continue with other aspects of the *Characteristics of Being Uncommon*.

SUPERHUMAN OR EXTRA INTELLIGENT?

One of the greatest obstacles to the recognition of extra intelligent people is the mysterious qualities and extreme rarity that many people (including parents) associate with "uncommon intelligence." Often it is either a kind of child-prodigy–assumption, like Mozart, or a comparison with other long-gone icons like Einstein and Madame Curie. The people that technically can live up to those expectations are indeed very, very rare. Perhaps 0.00003% of the population, 1 in 3.5 million, like the customary statistical benchmark for somebody who is officially called "profoundly gifted."[5]

But the group we want to discuss amounts to something like 2% of the population, that is, 1 in 50. (This is similar to the often-used benchmark for being labelled *gifted* in a specific IQ test.) Perhaps it amounts even up to 5% of the population, that is 1 in 20, if one would take the entire variety of multiple intelligences into account. Still rare – when considered within the specific domain of intelligence involved – but more common than most people are used expecting. However, the higher the degree of Xi, the better the characteristics of Xi will be recognizable.

All this means that many people will actually know one or more persons who are an XIP, without them being famous, notorious, or even conspicuous. However, often they are not recognized as XIPs. They lack these assumed mysterious "Einstein qualities," like the majority of XIPs.

> We remember talking to a manager of the civil service in a large city about our possible client, who we considered to be an XIP (incidentally, just like this manager we were talking to). He stated with certainty that there were no gifted people in his organization, and probably never would be either, since there would not be any adequate work for them.
> We managed to stretch his conviction only very slightly, mainly because he considered we could somehow be of value for his staff member.

In every million people, one may expect at the least 20,000 XIPs. They may work for all kinds of organizations, they may be volunteers, or even without a regular job. They may be TV-presenters, writers, all kinds of competent

---

[5] Profoundly gifted is the term for people with an IQ score higher than 175 on a standardized IQ test. See also chapter 4 in the section on *The degree of Xi*.

artisans, civil servants or entrepreneurs, politicians, sports people, marketers, architects, scientists, secretaries, or even janitors.
Their performance may be excellent, average, or far below average. XIPs may or may not be high achievers.
We do not claim that all XIPs have the innate ability to become the excellent master of their trade, let alone that they will all be effective and most successful.

However, we do claim that all XIPs have some uncommon qualities that are *special enough* to make a noted difference to themselves. They will also make a difference to their environment, if all involved are aware and ready to acknowledge the true situation.
These statements may feel like trying to navigate safely between cliffs and a violent vortex: Claiming that there is this really notable difference that needs to be taken seriously into account, while at the same time moderating exalted expectations of it. This issue is, however, a daily reality to many XIPs, and one of the reasons to consider the theme of *Enjoying the gift of being uncommon*, as I do in this book.

It seems to be an innate behaviour of XIPs to downsize their own qualities when comparing them to others. They *always* know many people who are far more intelligent or knowledgeable within a certain field of interest or proficiency than they are themselves. Ergo, they cannot be that special themselves, and by extension, they typically cannot be an XIP.
Typically, however, that same argument is also heard from these "far more intelligent people" they tend to refer to.
As a consequence, there are very few contemporary XIP role models who are allowed (and willing) to take on that role. Instead, we tend to get stuck with deceased, preferably undisputed, role models from various fields of science. The scientists who have won Nobel prizes, or generally speaking, discovered something most people have some difficulty understanding. This will not help us very much with identifying that 2-5% of the population.

The defining characteristics of an XIP, and the associated body of knowledge about uncommon intelligence, offer practical and down-to-earth tools to help discern these uncommon intelligent people more readily in everyday life. One of the reasons for this: It is far easier to discover their typical qualities without having unrealistic expectations. Is it not a tragic waste of assets to gaze in the distance in search of mythical talents, and overlook valuable uncommon talents right under one's nose, or in one's mirror?

If we accept XIPs to be a human variety, instead of being super humans, we can far more effectively enjoy their wealth of qualities. Neither do we have to be surprised about their number and their proximity to us.

Additionally, XIPs themselves will more readily acknowledge their being an XIP. It will help them to concentrate on exploring and applying their talents, instead of restraining them. Comments like "Who do you think you are, you're no Einstein, you know?" are not very helpful.

XIPs are definitely among us; let us welcome them!

A CONFUSING VARIETY OF DIFFERENCES

Many people have a tendency to assume that all uncommonly intelligent individuals strongly resemble each other.

It is only gradually, through meetings with our clients and through literature, that we have become aware of how immensely diverse this population of "uncommonly intelligent people" is.

As an example, see here the following fatal line of thought:

> *"He is clearly extra intelligent due to such and such characteristics. I don't have those characteristics to such a pronounced degree, so I cannot be an XIP."*

In reality, there is an enormous variety to be found among both the XIPs and gifted individuals: There are comparatively more ways in which one can be an XIP, than one can be *normally* intelligent (Tolan, 1999).

The two diagrams of figure 4 make this point more clear.

The left diagram shows the Gaussian- or normal distribution curve, representing the statistical distribution of IQ scores for a given test.

The height of the curve above the IQ score on the horizontal axis indicates how many people have such an IQ score, proportionally. The top of the curve, which correlates to the relatively largest number of people, is defined as the average IQ-score that is 100.

The uncoloured part to the right of the vertical line represents the group above the boundary value of 2%, the gifted individuals.
This (typical) representation gives the impression that this group of people is quite homogeneous, because they have a comparably high IQ. But it is actually the projection of an enormous diversity onto *one parameter* in a two-dimensional plane.

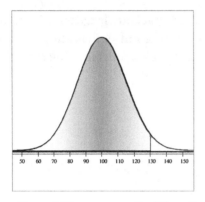
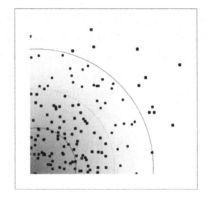

Figure 4: The same or quite different?

The right diagram illustrates how individually different the 2% exceptions are if we consider the projection of a *combination of two parameters* using a *two*-dimensional normal distribution: these are the dots in the white part, beyond the outermost circle segment. What these dots have in common is that they are widely separated from the centre which lies at lower left (the average, i.e. IQ=100), but they have little else in common. If this is the picture for a few areas of Xi, and so many areas exist, it is quite understandable how small the chances are of meeting an XIP whose "Xi-nature" resembles someone else's.[6]

---

[6] I leave open to discussion what the two axes really represent and whether this is sufficiently measurable: It is my intention that they indicate proficiency in any two different intelligences. One XIP can be an excellent pianist, but perform poorly in mathematics, another XIP vice versa. Both will recognize the various Xi characteristics for themselves, and both may consider the other the far more excellent one. That is, until they meet the pianist that is also proficient in mathematics, but not as proficient in sports like they are.
I already addressed the issue whether the group of XIPs really constitutes 2% or something like 5 % of the population, because there is no full correlation between the

It is the individuals who are relatively close to the centre who have a considerable chance of meeting someone who is intelligent in a similar way.

The diagram also illustrates how small the chance is that one's expectations of what an XIP can or cannot do will match identically with the XIP under consideration. XIPs tend to provide their environment (and themselves) with surprising qualities. This may work like birthday presents: The less precise the expectations about the presents are, the more disposed one is to joyful amazement and gratitude when the wrapping comes off.
And a further benefit is: The more an XIP will be stimulated to grow and develop himself/herself instead of trying crampedly and desperately to conform to expectations of a certain normed performance. See also chapter seven on Mindset.

Possible scenarios for acknowledgement

In this section we sketch the process of acknowledgement, spinning it out like a story, to make it more recognizable for all involved.

Someone who is extra intelligent is permanently so. Even when –for any number of reasons – he/she is not aware of being Xi, or has chosen to hide it in some way, it is still there.
Many XIPs have experienced the feeling of being different or out of the ordinary throughout their lives, and have managed to deal with this with varying degrees of success. However, a crisis may suddenly emerge, making it inevitable that something just has to be done. This can be the result of reaching a particular phase in life or of experiencing a particularly persistent feeling of dissatisfaction with the personal situation. The crisis can begin at work or at home.

- XIPs can come to the realisation at work that there is something not quite right with them that requires more thorough investigation. The employer or colleagues can recognise someone's Xi and draw attention to it.

---

different forms of Xi. However, whether it is 2% or 5% does not influence the main message of the graph: the extreme diversity within the – by definition – small group of XIPs.

- At home, the penny can drop through observing one's own children: What does their being considered different remind one of? Old memories are revived and the retracing of steps can lead to recognition of Xi, manifested in the children or in one or usually both parents. Alternatively helpful family members or friends can initiate the process of acknowledgement:
  "You were just the same when you were her age..."

XIPs at their workplace

XIPs learn quite early in their lives – sometimes even before they go to school – how to deal with the apparent *differentness* of their environment. These are emotional choices, whether to stand out more or to blend into the background. Many conclude, either consciously or otherwise, that they are better off not being labelled "highly intelligent," let alone "gifted." Some of these individuals achieve great things unnoticed, while others choose inconspicuousness and mediocrity. A third group drops out and performs extremely badly.

But here, too, the principle of "blood is thicker than water" applies.
If changes occur in the work situation or at home, or if a certain life phase induces a sense of restlessness, choices made in the past can be questioned and the opportunity can be taken to revaluate one's own qualities and to start using them.
Preliminary phases in the process of acknowledgement based on the work situation are:

- An escalation or outburst occurs which makes a change unavoidable.
- The employer or client wishes to implement major changes in the organization or in a project, and asks the XIP searching questions concerning their suitability and preferences.

An increasing number of employers are becoming aware of the link between behaviour and possible extra intelligence, and these employers are encouraging their personnel to investigate matters further. In practice, the relevant manager or HR officer often appears to have an affinity with the subject through family, friends or previous experiences.
The Health and Safety services and company physicians are also becoming

more knowledgeable about this subject, so that in specific cases of employee sickness a possible cause of the problems can be identified and a referral can be given for a more detailed investigation. The book, *Unguided missiles on course,* (Nauta & Ronner, 2007) – eleven case-studies with comments by a company physician and a psychologist – has helped a lot to achieve this. Giftedness has also been a topic at conferences of company physicians.

XIPs in their personal sphere

Because intelligence is, to a large degree, hereditary, parents, children, brothers, sisters, and grandparents are possibly just as intelligent as the XIP who is actively preoccupied with the topic. And yet acknowledgement is not always so obvious, because:

- Family tradition or gender prescribes a certain role;
- Everyone makes their own decisions concerning visibility of their uncommon qualities;
- The uncommon intelligence is not required or developed at school and in working life.

Children regularly cause parents to bring up the subject of Xi: Through "deviant" behaviour at school and/or the reaction of the school to this behaviour, past memories are revived. A surprising number of parents, and especially mothers, put in tremendous efforts to assist their children's development, without acknowledging their own possible extra intelligence. If they are Xi and acknowledge it, they will be in a better position to understand their child, and will also be a more consistent role model for them in the way they manage their being Xi and how they find their expression in the world.

Although the two partners in a relationship can be widely different in the make-up of their intelligence, it is very plausible that the true love of an XIP is also an XIP. Their mutual attraction is heightened by their shared need for intensity and complexity and by their shared drive.
But often the diversity of ways in which each of them may excel can complicate a correct estimation of the other's extra intelligence.
Certainly in the maternal line of parents, traditional role patterns often appear to have been effective in blocking the development of uncommon

intelligence. Solidarity with one's own dynastic line can then be a formidable obstacle in expressing one's intelligence fully in the present-day world.

Then there are of course the numerous Xi fathers who were not cut out for a school career. As imaginal thinkers or manual workers, they went into vocational training or straight into a trade. They may reach the top of their profession too early in their lives, sometimes accompanied by appropriate social success, or perhaps they will come unstuck in one-dimensional organizations run by one-dimensional managers.
When you acknowledge the treasure chest of exceptional qualities of your family, it will help you letting your own qualities and intelligences loose on the world. This subject is elaborated in chapter four in the section on Xinasty.

Family tree
Painting by Mariska Mallee

Chapter 2 *The Complexity of Being Uncommon*

CONCERNS ABOUT BEING DIFFERENT

As stated in the previous chapter, recognition of extra intelligence often involves more than a technical assessment of compliance with three or more of five characteristics. That is why we use the term "essential identification" with three or more of the five characteristics: It is more than a clinical statement, certainly for those who are encountering the notion of extra intelligence (Xi) for the first time, and who identify themselves with it. It is the combination of character traits, an apparent pattern, that surprises people, and occasionally even shocks them:

> *We have heard reactions from clients like:*
> *"How did you know that about me?"*
> *"It's 100% accurate!"*
> *"But everybody has that, don't they? (...I hope / I've always assumed)"*

The shock or relief is related to the unexpected confirmation of something that the speaker has known deep within himself/herself but has kept hidden too often:

> *"I'm somehow different from other people."*
> *"All my life I feel I have a secret."*

This realisation of "being different," certainly if this occurs at a young age, does little to instil a feeling of security in the individual. Many people therefore do their utmost to keep that feeling a secret, and try their best to behave *normally*. They acquire certain ideas why they just cannot be uncommonly intelligent, like:

> *"I often feel I am quite stupid."*
> *"I always had difficulties understanding mathematics."*
> *"I have not studied at an University."*
> *"I am far too lazy."*

Most often, after they have acknowledged their concern and emotions on the subject, XIPs are basically relieved to find out that their Xi is a most satisfactory explanation for many incomprehensible events in their lives.
Although it remains a very emotional topic, they ultimately do want to acknowledge their Xi.
In the section "Who does not want to be an XIP," I expand on four groups of reasons why someone may have an aversion to being an XIP.

Concerns expressed by others

Many people feel surprised or even shocked when they consider that someone they know might be an XIP. Mostly this is because their own implicit expectations of what an XIP looks and behaves like do not conform to their assessment of the XIP under consideration. These expectations may be inspired by a somewhat romantic notion of giftedness, as was already explained in chapter one.

But quite often the reason for their surprise or doubt is more trivial: Possible XIPs may have caused quite a lot of irritation in their environment by their behaviour and overall performance. Negative attention and the assumption that "something is wrong here," can be strong triggers for careful investigation. Thus when the conclusion tends to be that this rather difficult and unruly employee or family member is actually "very special," a typical XIP, one may still feel somewhat awkward about it. Should one, or should one not be glad or grateful with XIPs on the premises?

We have heard statements like:

> *"She may be an XIP or not, but I will not tolerate that she gives all kinds of unasked-for advice."*
> *"Lots of talk, but little of value coming out of those hands."*
> *"He cannot even write a decent report on simple issues!"*
> *"If she's so smart, why can't she manage her department properly?"*

The intriguing part of those comments is that often *blame may show the lead for fame*: (self-) reproach points to unique quality. The qualities that can be most distinguishing may be also the qualities that attract irritation and resentment, because they are so different from the usual, and/or are too exaggerated or not appropriate for that position or job. I will expand on this in the next chapter, about *the asset behind the nuisance*.

Acknowledgement brings relief at the workplace

In many cases, when XIPs acknowledge their extra intelligence, this results in a drastic difference in behaviour at their work. They have become more conscious of why and how possible conflicts may arise. They now understand and handle situations much better.
Naturally, their environment and their management appreciate this too. Their new attitude lowers the emotional barrier for acknowledgement on both sides, improving the situation even more. The organization derives more value from its assets; the XIPs can stretch and grow.
In other cases, XIPs definitely accept that their current job is a dead end and set out to find a different one. They are often facilitated by the organization that is willing to help now that the antagonism has subsided.

WHO DOES NOT WANT TO BE AN XIP?

Many XIPs are initially quite reluctant to consider the characteristics of Xi as possibly applicable to themselves, even when trusted relatives, friends or colleagues make clear that they do indeed feel strongly about the recognition. It is emotionally a very different situation whether one applies the characteristics to somebody else or to oneself.
In line with the already mentioned variety within the group of XIPs, the reasons for reluctance are also quite diverse. They may even be characteristical of certain facets of the Xidentity.

In our practice we have encountered at least four categories of arguments for reluctance to recognize and acknowledge one's own extra intelligence. Often a combination of categories is used:

1 Being linked to an exceptional group;
2 Having an uncommon intelligence;
3 Being your own authority to assess Xi;
4 Thinking the real problem must be more complex.

The first and second categories are often described in the literature on giftedness. The third category is different, because traditionally the label "gifted" can only be *awarded* to somebody by formal authorities. The fourth category may paradoxically be the result of the subject of uncommon intelligence becoming more accepted, as will be explained along with that category.

Being linked to an exceptional group

Some XIPs just do not experience being uncommon or atypical, or do not feel a need to make it explicit:

- They feel they belong in the first place to another group or organization, to their company, their family or whatever they strongly connect to. They do not perceive any added value in making marginal notes to that;
- Although their environment may unerringly recognize them as being a typical XIP, they will contradict it or keep their distance from the subject.

Others seem to have made a decision somewhere in the past to avoid situations or assessments of "being uncommon." This sentiment may be based on personal experience or on education. To designate oneself as *being uncommon* evokes strong emotions, for example:

- A feeling of horror, fear or grief for not sticking together with one's parents, other family members, or one's group;
- An abhorrence of the "logical" conclusion of having to feel superior to others;
- Anger and fear, because a carefully built reputation of "being normal" is about to become dismantled.

Some people resent the marking of differences between one human being and another. They want to underline the importance of what unites us all, and consider the laying out of differences between XIPs and non-XIPs as unnatural and counter-productive.

Humanity: The God with Thousand Eyes
Painting by Mariska Mallee

As I will explain in the next chapter about Ximension, we don't believe in conservation areas or other concepts of enduring separateness either. We don't believe that being an XIP implies superiority. But we also do not believe that denying perceived variety and diversity for principal reasons will be helpful to unite us all in a sustainable way.

Formula 1 race cars and mid-size sedans are both cars with four wheels. But they have different qualities to enjoy and they thrive in different environments. Similarly, one can enjoy the qualities and value of XIPs and non-XIPs alike. The uniting issue is how to enable both to express their unique qualities to their own advantage and to the advantage of our world as a whole.

Having an uncommon intelligence

The thought of possessing an uncommonly high intelligence is to many people highly incredible, to others frightening and sometimes it is both.
In the case of *incredibility*, people often have had negative experiences at school, or scored not too high (or even remarkably low) on IQ-tests.
Bad academic performance at school is emotionally linked to a stigma of ignorance or laziness or both. If such negative feedback was received in the past, it is rather odd to think of actually being extra intelligent.

Many people are convinced that uncommon intelligence automatically leads to excellent performance. If one is assumed to have an uncommon intelligence, this leads to the *frightening* thought of having to comply suddenly with very high performance standards of others (and of oneself). The seemingly safe strategy is to dispute one's uncommon intelligence, in order to keep one's fear of failure or low self-esteem manageable. As the saying goes: *"Play ignorant."*

Being your own authority to assess Xi

To many people it is an awkward task to assert one's authority to assess one's own extra intelligence. This may be caused by various reasons; we will mention two of them.

- *Prevailing opinions on authority and expertise*: To many people authority is necessarily linked to official authorities and certified experts;

- *Emotional insecurity*: Because XIPs are uncommon, their views and reactions may have led to disbelief and/or have given offence in the past. "Who do you think you are?!"

Feeling some doubts about one's Xi is not the real problem.
The real challenge is to stop confining one's doubts to an internal thinking process and to start communicating about the possibility to oneself and to others.

> *Sometimes it is stimulating to gather more knowledge about the subject and Ximension is definitely an effective environment in which to do so. Similarly it often works to write down all reasons why being an XIP is not applicable. Putting the doubts into words makes one realize that many arguments against being Xi do not cut wood.*
> *While in a group, this effect is even stronger; especially when you hear somebody else is expressing your own arguments who is, by your own observation and standards, a typical XIP.*

Thinking the real problem must be more complex

Recently a client explained that he did not want to put effort into investigating his uncommon intelligence, because he considered it to be a distraction from tackling his *real* problems.
In principle this can be very true of course.
In this case, however, his discovery that there existed an extensive body of knowledge about various issues that had been bothering him already for many years, led to the conviction that the solution could not be that simple. As the subject of extra intelligence becomes more easily accessible and accepted, it may paradoxically have this effect.

It is well known that XIPs may have difficulties with easy tasks, as they cannot imagine or perhaps accept that an authority seriously proposes something that obvious. They conclude that there must be some hidden meaning involved, and postpone the task to think about a clue first.
Their minds get stuck in a kind of thinking loop and the issue becomes more complex and often more worrisome.
Again, as in the previous category, gathering more knowledge, practising the findings, plus entering in communication with others, helps one to get into a

more perceiving mode. The use of one's senses for new input, instead of recombining previous convictions, promotes the search for practical solutions, and actually being an XIP can be one of them.

Of course there may also be other issues at stake – after all, XIPs are complex beings – but being aware of some typical characteristics of XIPs helps in sorting out priorities for action.

RECOGNITION THROUGH VEXATION AND REPROACHES

How bad is it not to be average? We often hear clients groan:

> *"Sometimes I wish I was simply normal."*
> *"Why can't I ever act like other people do?"*

Being average seems to be a desirable state to be in, if you're not normal yourself.

We have heard managers groan about XIPs:

> *"Why is she always in such complicated conflicts with her environment?"*
> *"Why can't he accept arrangements my other employees never complain about?"*

Being average seems to involve less trouble for managers.

I already mentioned some concerns about XIPs in the previous sections. Over the years we have collected a list that is much longer. It may not seem to be an advantage that XIPs can be recognized (and can recognize themselves) through the irritation they cause and the reproaches that are being made towards them. Rationally, however, is it the natural consequence of being different and using this quality in the wrong way, at the wrong place, or at the wrong time, or any combination of these. In the next chapter I will be more specific on how reproaches can be turned into compliments. In this section I will expand on characteristic reproaches to and vexing behaviour of XIPs interacting with their environment.

Characteristic reproaches

Since extra intelligence is by definition *extra*, XIPs who do their thing will attract special attention. The possible irritation or perplexity of their environment is usually linked to the relatively *extra* of whatever is happening. Almost always certain patterns will emerge, due to XIP's characteristic *intensity*, *complexity* and *drive*. These patterns were marked by Jacobsen (1999) as specially meant to put the XIP's nose back to the grindstone.

I slightly changed the criticisms as described by Jacobsen, and added the invoked sense of guilt. They are put together in Table 1:

Table 1: Top Ten criticisms and their implied sense of guilt

	CRITICISM	SENSE OF GUILT
10	Why don't you slow down?	I am impatient again.
9	Can't you just keep to one career direction?	I have to choose, or I will never make my way properly.
8	Why do you always have to do your things the hard way?	I'm overdoing it again; they must think I'm a loser
7	You worry about everything!	I should be minding my own business.
6	You are always so extremely sensitive and dramatic!	I am a proper nuisance. I should behave less sensitively.
5	Where do you find all these ideas?!	My imagination is running wild again; I should keep quiet!
4	You're so demanding!	I am being unfair again.
3	Can't you ever be satisfied?	I am ungrateful, I am asking too much.
2	You are always so driven!	I am pushing far too hard. I should not get myself so worked up.
1	Who do you think you are?	I'm doing things totally wrong again, me and my big mouth!

The table illustrates the way criticisms function with XIPs over the years.

When XIPs hear criticism, they automatically throttle down, because it is an unanswerable remark that evokes a sense of guilt. In fact, many XIPs have become convinced that the criticism is well deserved and that they should be ashamed of themselves. Some already step off the gas when they become aware that they are working at full speed, as they expect their environment will not appreciate it. I ordered the criticisms according to my estimation of their power to invoke guilt.

If many of these entries are familiar, either in the left or the right column, it is worthwhile to consider whether there is a case of someone being an XIP. This may open the possibility to turn this negatively inspired recognition into something advantageous.

Intense vexation

Unfortunately it must be said; some XIPs seem to have a talent for getting jobs at places that are "wrong" for them: In their urge to try to just be normal, they may enter organizations that cherish stability and adhere to formal rules as a natural and appropriate policy. After some time, they get bored or frustrated about this efficient "normalcy" and start to perform less, or begin to ask tendentious questions. If an organization tries to correct by more explicitly equalizing the XIP or by more control, it usually leads to fight or flight reactions of the XIP. When XIPs feel their innate quality to do things differently is not properly valued, they either start overdoing what they do, or become resentful. This is most certainly not welcomed. But XIPs can be very persistent and effective in vexing their environment until the entire organization is almost conspiring to stop and expel them.

More generally speaking: as long as XIPs don't know or don't acknowledge their special qualities and their being and doing *extra* in many respects, they get unsatisfying jobs, engage in unsuccessful personal relations and basically prolong their misconceptions.
Of course that is similar to what happens to all kinds of people, XIP or not. In the case of XIPs, however, their *extra*, and their innate *intensity*, *complexity* and *drive* make it more vehement, for them and for their environment.
That is one of the pragmatic reasons to recognize this characteristic for what it is and to want to do something about it.

Chapter 3 *The Challenge of Acknowledgement*

THE ASSET BEHIND THE NUISANCE

We already suggested, "Blame may show the lead for fame." That is to say that unappreciated personal characteristics might be hidden or distorted good qualities, which just need to be expressed differently or at a different time and place to become fully appreciated.

"You are always so driven!"
As an example: "You are always so driven!" clearly indicates irritation about apparent stubbornness, (too) strong ambition or the use of considerable pressure to reach goals.
The XIP may feel guilty about *again* being too pushy, forceful, or resolved and may decide to back down. But the XIP may also be aware of his/her growing irritation about the other's apparent slackness, wandering goals, conformism, or lack of devotion.
Instead of feeling guilty or irritated, the XIP may reply: "Yes, I do have my focused way of doing things, and there are lots of things that I intend to accomplish or move forward with." It is a truthful rejoinder but may also be interpreted as a reproach in return, with dubious consequences.

More positively, one should consider the fact that *drive* is simply a characteristic. It can be quite sought after at various locations or situations where a lot has to be done. It has even more value when coupled with a lot of attention to all involved aspects needed, executed in a tight timeline.
However, it may be the case that the present situation of the XIP is not one of those locations, and never will be, either.

But as long as XIPs are not inclined to realize and accept that their own seemingly "regular" drive has a specific *uncommon* quality in it, they may repetitively be unpleasantly surprised by the – in their opinion – remarkable lack of drive of their environment. And they will continue to react correspondingly to the disadvantage of both parties involved.

The ten criticisms revisited

The previous example can be extended to the other nine criticisms of the previous chapter. To give an impression of what that leads to, the right column of table 1 has been changed: *sense of guilt* is replaced by *special asset*. These assets are possible underlying reasons for the behaviour that gives rise to the criticism.

Table 2 intends to convey the added value of investigating beyond the irritation, even though this irritation may be completely justified. Any personal expression has always to be considered in relation to the context it is delivered in (as will be enlarged upon in chapter five and six).

Table 2: Ten criticisms and their unseen special asset

	CRITICISM	SPECIAL ASSET
10	Why don't you slow down?	High productivity.
9	Can't you just keep to one career direction?	Ability to transcend borders among various disciplines.
8	Why do you always have to do your things the hard way?	Acceptance of personal sacrifices to obtain excellent results.
7	You worry about everything!	Intensely caring, both for people and for one's work.
6	You are always so extremely sensitive and dramatic!	Excellent antenna for emotional undercurrents in organizations.
5	Where do you find all these ideas?!	Fruitful creativity.
4	You're so demanding!	Intense focus on activity.
3	Can't you ever be satisfied?	Motivated to hold high standards to obtain intense satisfaction.
2	You are always so driven!	Ability and perseverance for pushing the envelope.
1	Who do you think you are?	Capacity for not taking things for granted and striving for the best.

Excellent creativity is not much appreciated in the environment that has been tailored down to lean mass production, but may be of very high value to a company that is trying to innovate production methods. High sensitivity is not too practical in an emergency ward, but may work out excellently in complicated change processes of stressed organizations.

In conclusion, it is important that both XIP and environment are aware of the possible *extra*-ness of their assets, and that they are willing to acknowledge them. That may lead to finding means for fruitful expression within the organization or if necessary somewhere else.
Just consider that a strong asset that is not used in the long run tends to turn sour and to become a burden to all involved. It is definitely worthwhile to be aware of these signals and to pay attention to them.

THE UNDERLYING CHALLENGE OF DIVERSITY MANAGEMENT

Stating that XIPs are a minority that should be allowed equal opportunities to get a job and a promotion in due time seems an awkward way to promote their case.
Stating that XIPs have an abundance of assets, and that it is a shame and waste that society does not make a proper and effective use of this, raises the issue about expectations of performance that will be addressed in chapter six. Generally speaking, most XIPs do not flourish when they are prodded to perform in some prescribed way.

In fact, both arguments sound similar to statements that can sometimes be heard concerning the participation of cultural, racial or gender minorities in various companies and organizations. Are there other approaches to these issues of *diversity management* that can be useful to enhance acknowledgment of Xi?
I became interested in this approach through a meeting with Dutch colleague Grethe van Geffen and after reading her book on diversity management (Geffen, 2007). She started her own consulting company on diversity management 13 years ago and is also a very active member of Mensa Nederland.
I will give a short overview of the subject and then return to the possible application to XIPs.

Diversity Management issues

Diversity management has been a topic in literature and various management courses for a couple of decades now (Thomas Jr., 2006). Its main activities were driven by two very different lines of thought:

- *The business case*: Many companies and organizations operate in a global multicultural marketplace, where customers are very diverse in race, gender, age, and religion. If the company or organization has a workforce that represents to some extent this diversity, it can much better understand and accommodate its customers. It is in the company's or organization's own interest to strive for diversity and manage it.
- *The social justice agenda*: Companies and organizations have a moral and legal obligation to provide – as much as is possible – equal opportunities to all citizens, without discrimination by gender, race, religion, age or physical disabilities. Given the fact that society has become more diverse, choices about the composition of the workforce must follow.

Many companies put much effort in *representation* and *relationships*:

> *Do we have the right number of employees from all affected minorities, and can we encourage positive relationships among them in the workplace? Are we fulfilling our formal obligations and managing the continuity of our activities properly?*

A third factor, *paying attention to effective communication,* is always necessary. It needs, however, the increase of individual and collective awareness of and sensitivity to differences. This is sometimes felt to be at odds with the organization culture, expressed by (un)written statements like: "We must all have similar interests and ways of doing things, without discord or conflict." In any case it takes serious effort and craftsmanship to improve communication in a diverse population, but it is worth that effort. As is suggested in the business case, diversity management can create that promised extra added value for the organization.

The underlying challenge of diversity management therefore seems to be that managers are willing and able to *manage complexity* in order to be effective in a diverse, complex environment. As Thomas Jr. states in his article:

"The diversity focus will shift... to a craft for making quality decisions in the midst of differences, similarities, tensions and complexities." (p. 49)

Diversity management with regard to XIPs?

The cited perspective seems quite appropriate to improve the effectiveness of XIPs in organizations for these reasons:

- XIPs are a very diverse group as such, and most of them have a very diverse set of personal qualities. They are quite different compared to each other, and in another way different compared to normal intelligent people;
- Within almost all organizations XIPs form a minority and have to deal with the possible tensions that this may involve, just as the assumed majority and the management have to handle their position either implicitly or explicitly;
- XIPs have a natural affiliation with complexity, because they perceive many different levels of their environment simultaneously. They are inclined to communicate that complex view, when decisions for future actions have to be taken.

Allowing for diversity or complexity as offered by XIPs needs conscious effort: Promoting the average is often more practical or efficient. It also has the advantage of putting more mass behind its cause. Therefore in organizations, increasing efficiency is most often achieved by limiting variation, just as mass production is cheaper than custom building.
On the other hand, we can see in nature as well as in economics that accommodating some variety is a practical tool that has more adaptation potential in changing circumstances. Monocultures are vulnerable to external disrupting influences.

It is a practical fact that, due to their innate diverse and above average qualities, XIPs can be change agents in organizations. They may be able to foresee possible harmful consequences of current market actions that others cannot yet imagine. They will often be the first to make a growing organizational unrest visible, urged by their own high sensitivity for fairness and justice. XIPs are both helpful for, and helped by, a style of management that is actively striving to handle differences, similarities, tension, and complexity in an open way. They provide the practical illustration that diversity works as a sensor for and facilitator of the need to change.

Diversity allows organizations to deal more adequately with the growing complexity of their environment. In return, XIPs experience being valued for what and who they are, and are motivated to develop their natural assets in the most effective way.

One of the means to stimulate productivity and personal development of XIPs in organizations is to make conscious use of the special quality that interaction among XIPs usually has. That is the subject of the next section.

The possibilities of Ximension

It is a common experience of XIPs – sometimes to their astonishment or even embarrassment – that the interaction with other XIPs has a special quality to it. It is like accelerating and shifting into higher gear when picking up speed. It is often combined with a feeling of extra sensory input. Conversation becomes faster and more intense; mutual inspiration and association often follow. (By the way, the opposite can happen too, and just as intensely.) It occurs with colleagues at work and with complete strangers, young and old, male or female, with unexpectedly interesting meetings at parties and presentations or while travelling.

It has undoubtedly something to do with these characteristic qualities of *intensity*, *complexity* and *drive* of XIPs. They have a high level input of information coming from their senses, they process all this information rapidly and simultaneously, and they long to express all their findings, if possible, to their environment. When meeting other XIPs the interaction becomes immediately more multifaceted and more intense than with normal intelligent people. Somehow there is the experience that one's own qualities are mirrored unusually strongly in the other, as we will suggest in chapter seven in the section on Mirror Neurons.
But probably the most important aspect is the experience that one XIP can behave normally with the other. No need to slow down one's pace of thinking, to simplify conceptual complexity, or to mask one's intensity of feelings. What is usually extra somewhere else is normal here.

We have come up with a term to describe these situations: *Ximension*.

- Ximension is the dimension where being Xi goes without saying. It is an extra aspect of the living space of XIPs, geared to the "extra" of their extra intelligence;
- In Ximension practical and embodied knowledge about the qualities of XIPs is available, without judgment about their quantitative aspect. Therefore Ximension is a safe haven for inquiring about one's "uncommonness" and comparing it with others';
- Ximension is a place to stock up and recharge before returning to the normal world to live and express oneself amidst XIPs and non-XIPs alike. It is not a conservation area, where one can retreat to indefinitely;
- Ximension can be seen as a physical environment, but also as a state of mind.

Actively facilitating moments and places of Ximension is one of the managerial tools to stimulate effectiveness and personal development of XIPs in organizations. The practical realization can take all kinds of form and visibility, depending on the organization and the number of XIPs possibly involved.
The main issue is to be aware of the possible added value of Ximension and to create the opportunities to make it happen.

Innovative companies or centres of excellence tend to cluster in certain geographical regions, of course for infrastructural reasons, but also for the availability of an inspirational climate that attracts valuable personnel.
In those organizations it is considered normal to allow for various kinds of inspirational interaction, even if the participants are not working on the same project or in the same department.
They exchange information which may be unexpectedly helpful for their own work. Most often the process of hearing the other's story activates creativity to solve one's own work problems, thereby increasing productivity and effectiveness of both XIPs involved.

But the positive influence on personal development and self-confidence is also remarkable and worthwhile.

Ximension stimulates personal development

In the setting of Ximension it is well recognized and accepted that XIPs often needs to overcome certain inner barriers to perceive, acknowledge and bring into practice their own special qualities. Some XIPs just need feedback on and affirmation of their own suspicions about their Xi, while others definitely need help to come out of their own shadow.

In Ximension it is also accepted that the authority to acknowledge being an XIP lies with the XIP himself/herself. Likewise one's own senses will assist in discovering and experiencing *how* one is an XIP, or what one's Xidentity (see chapter four) looks like.

Many XIPs are more ready to accept their own being Xi after their experience of the unusual quality of interaction with others whom they consider obvious XIPs, in Ximension.

The challenge while being in Ximension is to allow oneself and the other to stretch and grow.

> *"On many occasions I have tremendously enjoyed discussions with you, who I consider to be a very intelligent person. You indicate that talking with me is very inspiring to you, due to my input and the speed and clarity of my reactions. I have come to the conclusion that this mutual experience almost forces me to accept that I must have an uncommon intelligence too."*

Conclusion

To sum up, Ximension can be experienced wherever two or more XIPs meet and allow themselves to be mutually inspired and supported.

It can be created in organizations that are willing to acknowledge the complexity of differences and similarities among their employees and that strive to benefit from it, for the sake of the organization and of all involved.

It can be found in any place where knowledge of extra intelligence is available, acknowledged, and shared.

It can certainly be experienced in our own career coaching practice, but likewise in other practices where this view about XIPs and their unusual qualities is put to work.

Ximension can also be created in the family, when there is support for *the way we do things here*, and for the diverse qualities of everybody's Xi. See also chapter four in the section on Xinasty.

And essentially it can be found in the mind of every XIP as an expression of inner recognition and acknowledgement of one's individual qualities, and of the openness to share this wealth with others.

GOOD REASONS TO ACKNOWLEDGE XI AND XIPS

Important choices like "Do I want to be an XIP?" or "Do I want to know whether this person is an XIP?" can of course also be assessed very pragmatically by starting from these points of view:

What is in it for me? What good will it do for me?
What good will it do for this person when I treat him/her like an XIP?
Will it lead to an increase of personal or organizational effectiveness?

It may help to consider the following questions:

Given the consideration:
Do I want to be an XIP?

- Can I think of another equally satisfying reason to explain my strong recognition of the given characteristics of XIPs?
- Will it offer a better explanation for all kinds of fortunate or unfortunate events in my life than continuing to assume that I am normally intelligent?
- Will it offer a more realistic and/or motivating frame of reference for my career development?
- Will it help me to better understand my preferences in choosing friends and relations?
- Will it show me ways to better understand my children, who seem to behave somewhat strangely at school, something I remember vaguely about my own youth?
- Will it help me to appreciate others if I understand myself better?
- Does the body of knowledge about XIPs explain the origin of certain personal qualities that I usually do not prefer to tell anyone about?
- Or, by indirect proof, what damage do I inflict upon myself by persisting to think that I am normally intelligent, while I actually am *extra* intelligent: Just an XIP, after all?

Given the consideration:
Do I want to know whether this person is an XIP?

- Can I think of another equally satisfying reason to explain my strong recognition of the given characteristics of XIPs?
- Will it offer a better explanation for all kinds of fortunate or unfortunate events in the curriculum vitae than continuing to assume that this person is *normally* intelligent?
- Will it offer a more realistic and/or motivating frame of reference for career development?
- Will it help me to better understand the person's preferences in choosing and cooperating with colleagues and relations?
- Does the body of knowledge about XIPs explain the origin of certain personal qualities that I like or do not like about this person?
- Or, by indirect proof, what damage do I inflict upon myself and my organization by persisting in thinking that this person is normally intelligent, while he/she actually *is* extra intelligent: Just an XIP, after all?

However, when all is said and done, it is always the personal choice of an XIP to believe or not to believe that he or she is an XIP and to accept the consequences. His/her environment can only respect this choice.

But this environment does also have the freedom to come to their own conclusions about the other being or not being an XIP, to use this knowledge to their advantage and accept those consequences.

PART TWO

THE SECOND PRACTICE: EXPLORING XI

Chapter 4 *Discovering Xidentity*

The first Practice, *Acknowledging Xi*, makes clear *whether* someone is uncommon, i.e., extra intelligent. It provides a base for the context of this gift of being uncommon and for awareness of the possible consequences.
The next question is: *How* is someone uncommon or Xi? Because there are so many possible forms of Xi, XIPs often discover only gradually what their specific variety of being uncommon is about.
The second Practice, *Exploring Xi*, addresses this question through the discovery of one's *Xidentity* (a combination of the words *Xi* and *identity*).

It is important to have a clear awareness about someone's Xidentity: It offers knowledge about one's unique possibilities, one's vulnerabilities and one's risks of becoming imbalanced or bogged down.
XIPs can be compared to a precision instrument; this Practice is about getting to know what it is and how it works, and about how to take proper care of its effective operation.
Xidentity specifies what kind of power and fragility one needs to manage. Using the power helps XIPs to express themselves in all their qualities. Taking their fragilities into proper account helps XIPs to make that expression sustainable, and contributes to personal development and well-being.

The nine facets of Xidentity
Xidentity is a collection of nine characteristic facets of extra intelligence that mutually influence each other. These nine facets can be used as focal points to achieve clarity about how someone is Xi.
Of course, Xidentity is not a complete blueprint of someone's personality; this would be a rather narrow view of the wealth of characteristics that every person possesses. Xidentity is a practical model for showing that extra intelligence is demonstrated through a variety of specific characteristics, which – in their combination and interaction – make XIPs who they are. It implies more aspects than just a high degree of one or more of the multiple intelligences.
We have developed the model of Xidentity in our own counselling practice by applying various available methods and concepts to all kinds of aspects of personal behaviour, in the context of extra intelligence or giftedness.

The facets of Xidentity are like lenses through which to look at yourself or someone else. They attract attention to a certain aspect of the personality that may be very characteristic of the way that someone is Xi. At the same time the facet facilitates awareness of the broad variety of other possible values or types of this aspect, which characterizes other XIPs in your environment.

The Model of Xidentity

While designing the schematic model of Xidentity (see figure 5), we wanted to express the fact that the nine facets mutually influence each other and that certain facets are more closely related to some facets than to others.

The four facets *extra receptivity*, *multiple intelligences*, *temperament* and *male/female archetypes* have in common that they are multiple and that an XIP draws his/her own "composition" from each facet.

The three facets *extraversion/introversion*, *imaginal thinking/verbal thinking* and *extra empathy/extra task-orientation* are polarities, with an XIP being located – or moving – somewhere along the continuum between the poles.

The central facet *degree of Xi* works as a reinforcing factor on the other eight facets. The stronger one's Xi is, the more extreme the character or expression of the facets will be.

We have chosen facets that are easily recognizable and to some extent verifiable by XIPs or their environment through observation and/or questioning. They are not necessarily mutually independent, as we have noticed various patterns of occurrence in our practice: But usually our clients feel attracted to specific facets to start their exploration because of their specific questions regarding their Xi.

The number of facets and the graphical representation of the Xidentity have changed since our first book that was published in 2007. It is plausible that the description of Xidentity will change again in the future, as we continue to discover certain aspects of the personality of XIPs that influence their behaviour in a different way than in the case of normally intelligent people.

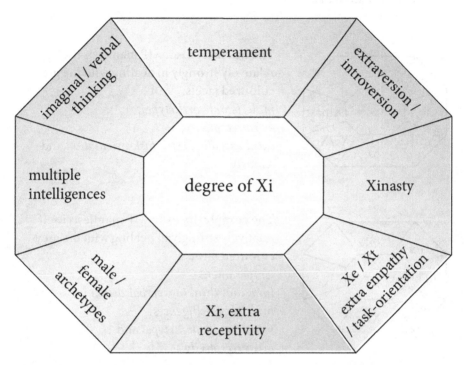

Figure 5: The Model of Xidentity

Additionally, the grouping of the eight facets around the central facet is linked to typical characteristics of XIPs as described in chapter one. In other words, linked to *intensity, complexity* and *focus* (this last being a more expanded formulation of *drive*).

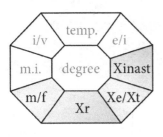

The **intensity** of an XIP manifests itself relatively strongly in dealing with the grey-coloured facets:
male/female archetypes,
extra receptivity,
extra empathy/extra task-orientation and
Xinasty.

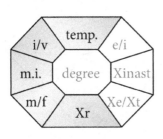

The **complexity** of an XIP manifests itself relatively strongly in dealing with the grey-coloured facets:
temperament,
imaginal thinking/verbal thinking,
multiple intelligences,
male/female archetypes and
extra receptivity.

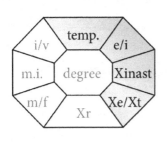

The **focus** of an XIP manifests itself relatively strongly in dealing with the grey-coloured facets:
temperament,
extraversion/introversion,
Xinasty and
extra empathy/extra task-orientation.

In the following nine sections, the various facets will be briefly described and explained.

MULTIPLE INTELLIGENCES

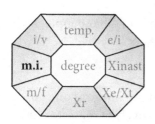

Howard Gardner (1999) has developed the concept of the multiple intelligences.

According to Gardner, intelligence is the ability to process information, and thereby to solve problems, invoke questions, or to create something that has value for the environment. All individuals, and, therefore, also XIPs, have at least eight different intelligences available to them through which they can express themselves. Gardner has described them as follows:

Verbal-linguistic intelligence
Being sensitive to spoken and written language, able to learn languages, and adequately using language to accomplish goals.

Logical-mathematical intelligence
Analysing problems logically, carrying out mathematical operations and performing scientific research.

Visual-spatial intelligence
Recognising and using the forms and patterns of wide space and more confined areas, spatial or two-dimensional, analysing graphically represented information.

Bodily-kinaesthetic intelligence
Using one's body or parts of it (such as the hand or mouth) to solve problems or to manufacture products. Having the ability to train and control one's bodily motions, coupled with a sense of timing.

Musical-rhythmic intelligence
Performing, composing and appreciating musical patterns. Having a feel for rhythm and melody.

Naturalistic intelligence
Observing, understanding, and organizing patterns in the natural environment. Being sensitive to the rhythm of the day and the seasons.

Having ability to recognise and classify plants and/or animals.

Interpersonal intelligence
Understanding the intentions, motivations and desires of other people, and thereby being able to collaborate effectively with others.

Intrapersonal intelligence
Having self-insight, an accurate self-image, including an image of one's own desires, fears and capacities. Using information effectively to regulate our own lives.

As an XIP, it is useful to ask yourself which of the intelligences are relatively strongly developed, and the extent to which their use gives you energy. It is often the case that school or work places a strong emphasis on your linguistic or logical-mathematical intelligences so that you can be "smart" when the occasion arises. Other strong intelligences may not have been taken seriously, or may have been dismissed as something for a hobby, possibly for later on in life.

But one or more of those other intelligences may well be a source of motivation and inspiration. Or it may even be that the waking up of one of those seemingly dormant intelligences will enhance the expression of the intelligence(s) that are currently used. There might also be a feeling of actually missing something, or not coming to full development, resulting in a loss of motivation and energy for the current activities or profession.
Sometimes the hobbies of an XIP may give a clue to intelligences that are as yet unused at work but could be also valuable there, while adding to a general sense of well-being.

IMAGINAL THINKING/VERBAL THINKING

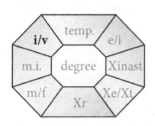

Imaginal thinking is thinking in a multi-dimensional associative structure of "images" in time and space. Often, the structure has visual aspects, hence the term imaginal thinking.

The image can be connected to sounds, feelings or other sensory impressions. In that case imaginal thinking is an associative structure of experiences, perceptions or pieces of imagination. Imaginal thinking is the way of thinking that includes our intuition and our creativity.[7]

Verbal thinking is thinking via a chain of words and notions, sequenced according to a logical structure. There is no obvious link to personal sensory impressions. It is the accepted form of scientific reasoning, and is associated with the left side of the brain.[8] Many XIPs can articulate their thoughts very well with words, thanks to a large vocabulary and a general proficiency in verbal thinking. It is one of the qualities that may give you an IQ score in the gifted range. But not all XIPs excel in verbal thinking.

We call someone an imaginal thinker who has a strong preference for imaginal thinking, and is relatively uneasy with verbal thinking.

XIPs are able to think in images to a great extent, but they are not always aware of this. Alternatively they may consider it as a kind of private/ personal thinking, because they have experienced that it is rarely possible to explain it to others. This is because an XIP thinks sensorially in relatively more dimensions and with huge leaps in thinking, which makes it difficult to explain those complex associative thoughts in the sequential manner of a discourse. But thanks to their intuitive powers, XIPs can often follow each other's cascading thoughts without having to use many words.

We have regularly noted that the higher the degree of their Xi, the more uncommon XIPs are in both verbal and imaginal thinking. While they all use the strongly associative and fast power of imaginal thinking in their creative

---

[7] Imaginal thinking can be connected to "visual-spatial learning" (Silverman, 2002).
[8] We have chosen to use the term "verbal thinking," because that opposes relatively clearly with "imaginal thinking." One may also rightly call it "thinking in notions," "sequential thinking" or "concept thinking."

processes, some are proficient in devising concise notions to describe their images, others are very able to express and explain their ideas and conclusions in words. Hearing themselves talk while explaining their ideas, can in fact stimulate their creativity too, leading to a new cycle of imaginal and verbal thinking.

Imaginal thinking can be accompanied by some form of dyslexia or dyscalculia. Because XIPs process information so quickly and may have built a massive library of (word) images in their memory, they are often able to mask this. But as a consequence they perform unremarkably in these areas. *Verbal thinking* can be accompanied by an inclination to rationalize everything, and with not being able to connect to, or properly value, one's feelings and emotions. This may impede one's ability to make decisions, reducing personal effectiveness.

The inexplicable right answer

Imaginal thinking happens at high speed, usually with a frequency of some 32 images per second. This is so fast that our brain is unable to consciously observe each separate image. This does happen, however, on an unconscious level. Therefore, the result of the thinking process appears all of a sudden and as a surprise; you do not know how you got there. At the same time, you are almost certain that your answer is the right one, because you have unconsciously followed your train of thought. It can be a puzzling experience for the XIP too, and may invoke one of the earlier mentioned characteristic reproaches expressed by others: "Where do you find all these ideas?!"

Three essential differences

Our friend and colleague, Mechel Ensing-Wijn, specializes in knowledge development and practical application of imaginal thinking. She has developed a clarifying comparison between imaginal thinking and verbal thinking. Her initial explanation was put forward in the paper: *Everything flows...* (2006). It was validated two years later by P. Edelenbos in a research study (as yet unpublished) that needed to describe and identify imaginal thinkers. I will describe her approach and add my own illustrations of the process of imaginal thinking and verbal thinking.

In addition to the difference of thinking in images versus thinking in words and notions, there are three essential differences between imaginal thinkers and verbal thinkers in the way that they process their information:

1. *Holistic/sequential thinking:* Imaginal thinking combines all kinds of subjective experiential information in a holistic flow of associations. Verbal thinking is essentially sequential and usually adheres to a logically acceptable, objective structure.
2. *Orientation in space/time:* Imaginal thinking is connected to movement without limitations. Visual images are mostly in three dimensions instead of two. The sense of time is related to movement and processes, not to digital clocks and being exactly on time.
   Verbal thinking follows sequences in time and is examining meaning and delimitations of words and notions. The agenda is a typical product of verbal thinking.
3. *Going with/against:* Imaginal thinking is flow-like thinking. (Hence Ensing-Wijn's title: *Everything flows…*) Like the river that is flowing, the thoughts are never the same, because they are connected to current sensorial input or recollections. The movement is divergent, outward oriented. Verbal thinking is convergent, oriented toward a centre. By halting the movement and by focusing, objects and concepts can be more accurately analyzed and described.

Imaginal thinking is metaphorically illustrated in figure 6: a garden sprinkler in action. When properly fed, a garden sprinkler will disperse this input in its own fashion, but always in a divergent way, adding new forms of content to the context where it is currently situated. The upper left image shows the importance of anchoring the sprinkler securely in the earth by means of its spike. If not anchored, the sprinkler will move chaotically and haphazardly. Everything just gets wet without a relevant purpose. The lower image conveys the additive effect of two imaginal thinkers on each other: They inspire each other without censoring, having their own dispersal pattern. Figure 7 illustrates schematically how two verbal thinkers discuss by gradually focusing in on each other's statements. By specifying what is different and what is similar in both statements, they find out what they can agree on: a converging process.

Figure 6: The diverging process of imaginal thinking

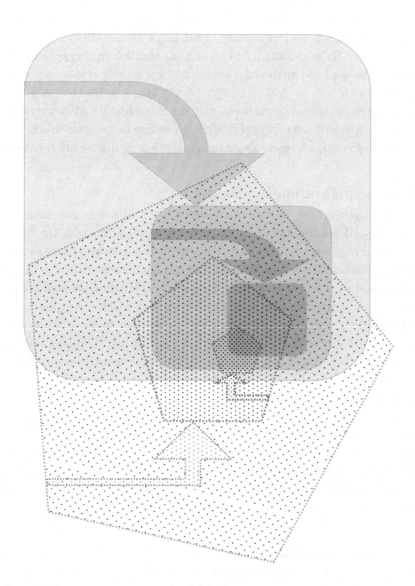

Figure 7: The converging process of verbal thinking

A discussion is typically a verbal thinking activity, just like brainstorming is the typical imaginal thinking one. The fascinating thing is that adding new information, a creative, free moving input, helps discussions that get stuck. And similarly, if the abundance of ideas from a brainstorming session is not properly assessed and analyzed – anchored – the wealth of ideas will flow on and disappear.
In organizations verbal thinkers can play the role of devil's advocates very effectively, but without imaginal thinking there can be no innovation.
There is, however, a fragility about imaginal thinking that needs attention:

The incomprehensible explanation
Imaginal thinkers "see" an idea or a solution to a problem in their mind. They can walk around it in their thoughts, sit in the middle of it, etc. Every way of looking at it provides another aspect of why it is a good idea or a good solution. But how do you explain something like that in words?
Imaginal thinkers will usually start the spoken explanation somewhere in their current spatial thinking structure. While they are choosing the right words for their story, and forming the right sentences, they are constantly being bombarded with images of other relevant aspects. This leads to sentences not being completed, the perspective of the explanation shifting unannounced, and finally to the audience giving up trying to follow it, to everyone's great frustration.

There is a practical solution to this inconvenience: Imaginal thinkers should try to explain their perspectives one at a time. They may switch to another perspective only after mentioning that they are going to switch. And they should be well aware to have the spike of their sprinkler firmly rooted in the ground. That prevents becoming suddenly chaotic.

The advantage of Ximension
Because imaginal thinking XIPs think in relatively more dimensions, this normally demands even more of their ability to explain clearly. In conversations with their peers in Ximension, however, both parties communicate in "imaginal thinking mode" and are able to associatively replicate the other's thinking processes.

It may also happen that one of those peers is more proficient in conveying the exchanged ideas appropriately in the organization. This boosts creative output in a very effective way, and prevents the creative imaginal thinking XIP from becoming sadly isolated in the organization.

Temperament

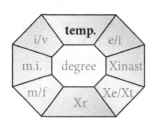

Temperament theory was introduced by Hippocrates in 370 BC and through the centuries has taken various forms and had varied degrees of popularity.

It is founded on the idea that four essentially different personality patterns can be distinguished.

American psychologist, David Keirsey, introduced in his book, *Please Understand Me* (1978), a link between Temperament theory and the Myers-Briggs Type Indicator (MBTI), and called the four temperaments Artisan, Guardian, Idealist and Rationalist. In the last 20 years American psychologist and prolific author, Linda Berens (2006), has made various additions to Keirsey's concepts and recently renamed the four temperaments in the context of their specific role in organizations as: Improviser, Stabilizer, Catalyst and Theorist.

I will use Keirsey's terms, as they are still the best known.

The usefulness of temperament theory for XIPs lies in the linking of temperament to personal drives/motivations and values, making the effects of their possible developments visible in a comprehensive way.

Of course, classification into four temperaments is a rough and ready method, but the four temperaments are so fundamentally different that this rough division still proves to be useful. It may occur that XIPs in our practice discover that they actually fit with another temperament than they had always thought and acted upon.

There are different approaches to distinguishing the temperaments. In this description, intelligence is chosen as the distinguishing factor.

I have put the most characteristic aspects of the four temperaments in one overview in figure 8 for easy comparison.

Artisan, Guardian, Idealist, Rationalist

ARTISANS possess *tactical* intelligence; they work on applied Mastery with both feet on the ground. They are practical, charming, in the here and now, love to improvise, are decisive, and aim to achieve maximum effectiveness in everything they do. They hate being bored and like to keep all options open.

GUARDIANS possess *logistic* intelligence; they are good at thinking up rules, procedures, schemes and such, and at sticking to them. They aim to be timely prepared for what can be expected of them and are experts in creating organizational stability. They try to fit in and adopt socially correct behaviour based on solid knowledge, preferably backed up by qualifications. They trust hierarchical structures.

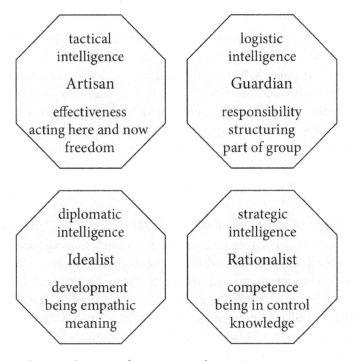

Figure 8: Overview of temperament characteristics

IDEALISTS have *diplomatic* intelligence; they focus on people and concern themselves with the deeper meaning of their own thinking, feeling and behaving, as well as that of others. Their strong points are their ability to reflect, their self-awareness and empathy. They would like everyone to develop in his/her very own way.

RATIONALISTS have *strategic* intelligence; they are able to oversee innumerable long-term possibilities in a calm manner, determine their strategic goal and take the most efficient path to reach that goal. They are allergic to constantly recurring mistakes, are creators of science and are competent "chess players" in mentally complex situations.

EXTRAVERT/INTROVERT

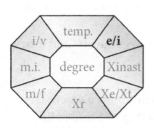

When Jung was developing his theory of psychological archetypes in the 1920s, he considered the relation between the individual and his environment as one of the characteristic factors. He distinguished *extraversion*, oriented towards the outside, and *introversion*, oriented towards the inside. The distinction between the two lies in the gradations in preference: An extravert can therefore also occasionally display introverted tendencies, and vice versa.

Extraverts are assumed to form the majority (65%) in the United States. This is why many people associate introversion with being a disorder, having a lack of communication skills, displaying anti-social behaviour, being depressed, and the like (Laney, 2001).

Introversion occurs much more frequently (50% and more) in XIPs (Silverman, 1998) but in various guises:

- On the one hand the "normal" introversion, i.e. a strong tendency to look inwards, from "still waters run deep" to noticeable shyness in company;
- On the other hand, a strong intuition or a sensual extra receptivity can lead to introverted characteristics, while the person in question is fond of the company of others – something that is typically linked to extraversion.

Many XIPs are equipped with a strongly developed intuition so that they are able to assess the moods prevailing within a group of people at a certain time. They may find it difficult to cope with this, either due to the amount of information or the type of information they are picking up on. It is as if they are being filled with impressions, or they lose contact with themselves as a result of all the information that is reaching them. In other words, they have the need to isolate themselves in order to assimilate all these impressions, or to get back into contact with their own energy supply.

This is the behaviour that is generally associated with introversion and when completing assessment questionnaires, this leads to the conclusion that one is introverted. If the person involved indicates appreciation of the company of others and after "recharging the batteries" immediately goes in search of company, then we can talk of an extraverted need. This should lead to a different conclusion about possible career paths, one of the reasons to consider this facet more closely with XIPs.
Here follow some tips for the communication between extraverts and introverts:

- Introversion is not a defect or a shortcoming or a disability as such. It is important that extraverts accept this, even though they can find it difficult to imagine what it is like to be an introvert. Do not try to make introverts more sociable;
- Extraverts want to make decisions immediately, because they make their decisions with the aid of interaction with the company of that moment. Introverts need to sleep on things, but after that they are convinced of their decision. It is important for an introvert to make clear that he/she needs that extra time; this it is not a sign of insecurity or indecision;
- Many of the differences can be explained by a preference for
  much, often, broad and immediately, versus
  little, now and then, deep, and after a break.
  Give each other space, or allocate the roles in such a way that both parties benefit;
- An extravert has the need to exchange ideas with more than one person. This is not a sign of "unfaithfulness" or a lack of self-confidence;
- Do not embarrass an introvert in public.
  Be aware that introverted discretion can be experienced and interpreted as scheming behaviour by an extravert.

Xinasty

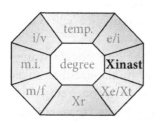

The novel concept of Xinasty is a combination of Xi and dynasty.

A dynasty is a ruling family. By using the term Xinasty we want to convey the idea that there often appears to be an implicit prevailing notion about Xi within a family, including ancestors. Such a notion can work in a severely restrictive way regarding the acceptance of, and dealing with, one's own Xi, certainly if that notion is not a consciously made one.

The "birds of a feather flock together" effect results in Xi couples being formed. Given the strongly hereditary component of Xi, there is often a majority of family members in which Xi characteristics can be observed, even if their expression can take extremely divergent forms. This may have been a process already going on for generations, but need not necessarily have resulted in scientific or social prominence. Even so, all the individuals involved have had experience with the feeling – either consciously or unconsciously – of being *different* from the average person, and they have made their own choices about how to deal with this.
This may involve inhibitory convictions like:

"Make sure you never get noticed" or
"Take it easy, otherwise it might be dangerous,"

or normative life rules such as

"You can't make a silk purse from a sow's ear."

It may also have resulted in the creation of a strong and enjoyable *Ximension* within the family, where expressing one's talents is naturally encouraged. Clients have told us stories like:

"In our family we often did things a bit different compared to many other families. It was never suggested that either way was better; our parents said it was just their preferred style."

Confusion about gifted and non-gifted

The classical definition of being gifted is often a confusing factor: Excellent performance at school or during a study is considered as being a necessary criterion for giftedness.

Failing at school leads to a lifelong judgement of "not being particularly intelligent." For example, a strong capacity for imaginal thinking, either linked to dyslexia or not, or a strong psychomotor extra receptivity (not being able to sit still at school) leads to dropping out or to being relegated to vocational education. This often occurs in more than one member of the family and can result in a prevailing notion that "our kind of people" just isn't that intelligent.

Another example within a family is: One child turns out to be the smart one at school, while the others are more interested in music, drawing or other "hobbies", or in networking with a chosen few of their own age.

Of course these others are not considered gifted, only that "smart at school" child is. Often negative reference is made in this context to characteristics of "ungifted" uncles, aunts, grandparents, etc. This can have a stigmatising effect on such a child.

One of its possible effects was described in chapter two: not being able to accept having an uncommon intelligence, and rejecting the idea of being an extra *intelligent* person. Being an extra *intense* person can be more attractive then.

When a son or daughter is labelled by others as possibly being gifted, or, for that matter, not gifted, these types of experiences can lead to vehement responses from their parents. Such a strong reaction does not leave the child unscathed, and thus the pattern continues.

The typical female and male line

A separate subject within this facet concerns the notions within a Xinasty about what is typical for the masculine line, and what is typical for the feminine line. For centuries, the prevailing conviction has been that women are naturally less intelligent than men, and that therefore giftedness in women actually does not exist, with a few exceptions proving the rule. Given the conviction that giftedness has to be proven by notable public achievements, few women at the time were in the position to prove their point (Silverman, 2006).

These days, many women still have difficulty in accepting that they may be Xi, while they do recognise the extra intelligence in their male partner or in their children. Given the difference between male and female archetypes, as will be discussed later on in this chapter, one can safely assume that typical feminine excellence is different but certainly of equal value to typical masculine excellence. This may also apply to the kind of interaction that is established and favoured in Ximension.

Extra empathy / task-orientation

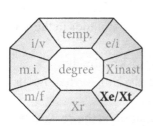

There are various typologies for personal or management styles that distinguish between "task-oriented" versus "people-oriented" focus. It is a way of assessing whether in your daily life and behaviour you particularly focus either on optimally fulfilling a task in terms of content, or on the people with whom you are connected in some way. We specify the concept of people-orientation as *ability to empathize – empathy –: the ability to place yourself mentally or emotionally in the shoes of another person.*

Because one of the characteristics of XIPs is their tendency towards limitlessness (they are naturally intense and driven), their personal characteristics often appear to be larger than life. It is then sometimes problematic trying to estimate when that "extra" gets the upper hand and becomes "too much" or even "pathological." Therefore if some XIPs, compared with other XIPs, are relatively task-oriented or relatively empathic, this means that their environment will actually perceive them as *extra task-oriented (Xt)*, or *extra empathic (Xe)* respectively. Dependent on the interchange with their environment, extra benefit is achieved, or an escalation occurs whereby the behaviour of the XIP is regarded as undesirable or even a disorder by the environment or by an expert.

How much *extra task-orientation* and *extra empathy* actually differ from each other is shown when the typical characteristics are compared. When both parties become involved in a relationship at work or in private life (opposites attract) they tend to have difficulties in accurately assessing the unfamiliar characteristics in the other party and in optimally dealing with them. In discord situations, this tension can easily lead to escalation as the *extra task-oriented person* has the tendency to become "*extra* extra task-oriented" – *XXt* – and the *extra empathic person* to become *XXe*: "*extra* extra empathic." In the terminology of the Core Quadrants[9]: exaggeration of the quality leads to too much of a good thing, and thus to a distortion. An allergic response to this distortion is the result, which has the effect of maintaining the distortion.

Seven characteristics of Xt and Xe

CHARACTERISTICS OF BEING EXTRA TASK-ORIENTED (XT):

- The plan or the task must be executed and anything that stands in the way of achieving this is by definition less important;
- There is a strong need for structure to execute the task optimally;
- People are assessed on their actual words and deeds. Non-verbal signals play little or no role;
- There is a strong ability to deal with concrete situations at the cost of an ability to generalize experiences;
- Over-stimulation of the senses of an extra task-oriented person easily leads to intense agitation;
- There is little tolerance for behaviour in the environment that does not comply with the XIP's own task-orientation;
- The extra task-oriented person feels uncomfortable with political games or other situations in which someone's words and deeds do not immediately reveal their intention.

CHARACTERISTICS OF BEING EXTRA EMPATHIC (XE):

- Extra empathic people cannot, in practical terms, switch off their empathic capacity;
- Extra empathic people have the tendency not to make a conscious distinction between their own feelings and those of another person they have tuned into,

---

[9] The Core Quadrant (Ofman, D. 1995, *Core Qualities, gateway to human resources*) describes personal characteristics based on the interaction of two complementary characteristics, Core Quality and Challenge, and their respective exaggerations, Pitfall and Allergy.

- What the other person thinks or feels is more important than what he/she does;
- The processing of information about the other person gained through tuning in to that person can easily suppress the processing of extra empathic people's own thoughts and feelings;
- Extra empathic people quickly feel responsible for another person;
- The need to help the other can be at the expense of doing things that are important for extra empathic people themselves;
- It is painful if the other person does not demonstrate any empathy.

Note that the characteristics are extra distinguishing because the natural intensity of the XIP constantly magnifies them slightly, making the consequences even more radical. This becomes all the more evident when the Xt/Xe gets extremely strong or exaggerated, as described hereafter with the *extra* version of extra task-orientation and extra empathy – *Extra* extra task-orientation (XXt) and *Extra* extra empathy (XXe).

Characteristic imbalances of XXt en XXe

In a state of *Extra extra task-orientation (XXt)*, extra task-oriented people will narrow and limit their focus, lose their overview, and become overloaded with fears of miserably failing on the task. They may get stuck in very non-effective or even offensive behaviour towards their environment, including high emotional peaks.
The environment can categorise their behaviour as that of typical for somebody with Asperger's syndrome or other variants of the autism spectrum. That is the pragmatic reason for why it is helpful for *extra task-oriented people* to be aware of their typical characteristic, so that an escalation spiral can be acknowledged and alternative actions can be debated: from *Extra XtP* back to *XtP*, reviewing the task in a broader perspective of various interests.

In a state of *Extra Extra Empathy (XXe)*, extra empathic people will focus completely on the other person, making their persistent care and attention a claustrophobic experience. They feel completely responsible for the well-being of the other person, while guiltily aware that they fall short constantly. As a consequence of their plummeting self-esteem, they lose their own feeling of personal authority, their capacity to take initiatives and in the end, their identity.

For the environment, the behaviour of extra empathic people acquires the characteristics of co-dependence and other forms of overdependence. That is the pragmatic reason why *extra empathic people* should be aware of their quality, so that they can recognise when imbalance and exaggeration is in the process of getting the upper hand. If extra empathic people are then able to devote attention, consciously and in a focused manner, to their own feelings and needs once again, they can revert from *Extra XeP* to *XeP*.

Effectiveness in work and relationships

Basically, being extra task-oriented or being extra empathic are attractive properties both in human terms and commercial effectiveness. However, if one's Xt or Xe gets out of hand, or is always strongly evident, this may lead to stagnation.

Through a better understanding of the various factors for escalation and of the process for de-escalation, one can use this quality in a more effective way. This includes awareness on whether one's own extreme behaviour appears to be situational – it does not occur or become problematic in many other situations – or that a high degree of Xt or Xe is more or less a constant characteristic.

EXTRA RECEPTIVITY

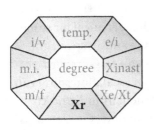

It is a fact that extra intelligent people experience life in an unusually intense manner: They are extremely interested in new developments, very concerned with others, or just as strongly introverted, have an outspoken taste in food, clothing or interior design, an extremely vivid imagination, exceptional or extremely outspoken ideas, and so on.

The average environment considers all this somewhat extreme on occasion, sometimes irritating and almost always astonishing. Conversely, the XIP can be surprised or become agitated when met with resignation, uncritically conventional behaviour, detachment or watered-down ethics on the part of others.

The Polish psychiatrist Kazimierz Dabrowski (1902-1980) developed a striking theory of personal development (Piechowski, 2006).
He considered intense inner restlessness or conflict to be a normal phase in psychological growth, whereby the hereditary and socially acquired values and convictions are transformed into a personally structured ideal system.
In Dabrowski's "theory of positive disintegration," he proposed that the disintegration of old, less-evolved structures leads to the forming of a new and more complex personality that can envision and create a highly conscious life. He noted that those who are capable of forming higher-level values would have an inborn extra-sensitivity of the nervous system; reactions to certain external stimuli occur more readily, are more intense and last longer than considered normal.
Dabrowski called this psychic state O*verexcitability*.[10]
We have introduced in our practice the term *extra receptivity* ("extra ontvankelijkheid" in Dutch), and found out that our clients could easily identify with this approach.[11]
Five areas of extra receptivity can be distinguished:

- Psychomotor;
- Sensual;
- Imaginational;
- Intellectual;
- Emotional.

Dabrowski considered *emotional extra receptivity* as the dominant driving force in the process of positive disintegration.
Someone who is extra sensitive in three or more areas (who is *extra receptive* for short) experiences reality essentially differently than the average person would: that is to say more intensely and more multi-facetedly.
This has a positive side to it, but also a difficult one; one can experience intense joy, compassion, or innovative creativity, but also intense sadness or frustration about "the state of the world."

---

[10] The English translation of the original Polish term meaning "Superstimulatability."
[11] We associated *overexcitability* with laboratory experiments or with irritability. For us, *extra receptivity* is about a personal characteristic one can take advantage of, and use it to deal with the disadvantages in a pragmatic way.

Personal growth and development can be viewed as the royal road to achieving a net positive effect of the extra receptivities. Without that consideration, extra receptivity will typically be seen as deviant or irritating by the people involved and by their environment. Because many XIPs have a high extra receptivity (Xr) in more than one area, far more than normal, this offers a partial explanation for their feeling different so often.
Additionally, the impact of this intensity on their high abilities in various cognitive processes gives rise to a qualitative different output. They not only have *more* imaginational or thinking power, but the results are in a kind of different key, compared to individuals of normal intelligence.

Being aware of the strengths and weaknesses of one's own Xr is a very important factor in the effective management of being uncommon.

Summary of extra receptivity
As inspired by (Piechowski, 2006, pp. 24-25).

Psychomotor extra receptivity
- Excess of energy;
  talks quickly, noticeably excited, intensive physical activities, strongly geared towards action (organizing), extremely performance-focused.
- Psychomotor expression of emotional tension;
  compulsive talking or chattering, acting impulsively, nervous behaviour (twitches, nail-biting), workaholism.

Sensual extra receptivity
- Heightened sensual and aesthetic sensation;
  enjoys seeing, smelling, tasting, touching, hearing and sex;
  is thrown into ecstasy by beautiful objects, forms or colours, melodious language or music and harmony.
- Sensual expression of emotional tension;
  over-eating, losing oneself in sex, attacks of spending mania, constantly wanting to be in the limelight.

IMAGINATIONAL EXTRA RECEPTIVITY
- Heightened powers of imagination;
  easily able to visualise spatial concepts, scenarios and processes.
  Experiences free imagining intensely. Little tolerance for monotony.
- Can live in a fantasised reality;
  own imagined world as a safety valve in situations of emotional tension.

INTELLECTUAL EXTRA RECEPTIVITY
- Intensified brain activity;
  curiosity, concentration, avid reading, keen observation, detailed visual memories, elaborated plans.
- Passionate poser of profound questions, and problem solver;
  in search of the truth and new concepts.
- Contemplative thinking;
  very fond of theory and analysis, intensely occupied with logic, morality, self-examination, integration of concepts and intuition, free thinking.

EMOTIONAL EXTRA RECEPTIVITY
- Intensified feelings and emotions;
  positive, negative, complex, emotional extremes;
  identification with other people's feelings,
  the awareness of a broad range of feelings.
- Strong physical manifestations;
  a knot in the stomach, losing courage completely, blushing,
  standing with a throbbing heart or with sweaty hands.
- Strong expressions of feelings;
  inhibition (fear, shyness), enthusiasm, ecstasy, bliss, pride,
  a memory strongly influenced by feelings, shame, feelings of unreality,
  worries and fears, guilt feelings, preoccupied with death,
  depressive and suicidal moods.
- Capacity for strong attachments and profound relationships
  with people, living objects and places; compassion, empathy.
- Keenly acknowledged feelings about themselves;
  inner dialogue and self-judgement.

Chariot of the Sun-God.
Glass object by Annelien van Kempen.
My favourite item in her 'Cars' collection for its radiant colours. For me it was immediately connected to my mental image of the Sun Chariot. Being a chariot, the link to the Warrior archetype is strong too.

Goddesses: Lady of Anatolia and Artemis
Glass objects by Annelien van Kempen.
Her recent inspiration for these kinds of forms relates to her interest in the archetypes of the goddess in various cultures and through time.

Male/Female Archetypes

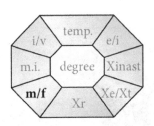

In the earlier section on Xinasty, I discussed how rigid role conceptions about masculine and feminine can act as a hindrance to expressing one's Xidentity. Deep convictions of the family involved, as well as of their environment may lie at the foundation of this. Archetypes are useful in making these thinking and behavioural patterns more explicit. They provide some handles to seeing the direction in which a change can be found, and helping to bring it about.

The approach is based on Jungian concepts of Animus and Anima, and on the work of Moore and Gillette (1990).
They put forward that the male psyche is built up of four essential aspects, archetypes. These four aspects (King, Warrior, Magician and Lover) can assume different guises, depending on the personal development of a specific person. The four named archetypes represent the form the truly mature man assumes. However, each archetype has two dysfunctional shadow forms – an active and a passive shadow pole – that can effectively block the expression of excellence.
Although there is various literature on characteristic female archetypes, I could not be satisfied with the ones proposed. Thanks to discussions with our colleague Amanda Bouman, I was able to come up with – in my opinion more complementary– female counterparts of the male archetypes and choose names for them. The resulting extensive model is presented here in a condensed form.

The practical use of this facet of Xidentity is to identify shadow poles and mature archetypes that fit significantly and give extra insight into strengths and possible areas of development. Please note that a woman can identify with male archetypes too, and vice versa.
Secondly, XIPs will find it practical to limit themselves to one or two archetypal aspects that are most recognisable for them *and* that seem attractive for them to focus extra attention on.

As an overview, table 3 contains the full model. For each aspect, we will expand briefly on the female and male form and their shadow poles, and on their relation with Xi.

Table 3: Female and male archetypes

Shadow ±	Mature female	Mature male	± Shadow
Overprotecting +	Protectress	Warrior	+ Sadist
Indifferent −			− Masochist
Poisoner +	Nurturer	Magician, Shaman	+ Detached Manipulator
Barren field −			− Denier
Pushover +	Hostess	Lover of life	+ Addict
Noncommittal −			− Depressive
Control freak +	Director	King	+ Tyrant
Absentee −			− Weakling

Protectress and Warrior

The Protectress and the Warrior concern the use of power and aggression. In Xi terms, this is about drive. Both are driven by an inner value system: a mission.

The *Protectress* knows what is of value and will not hesitate to unconditionally safeguard this with passion and all of her might.
The shadow poles *Indifferent* and *Overprotecting* protect too little or too much, causing losses or a fearful rigidity.
The *Protectress* will safeguard an XIP's Xidentity as well as finding the right balance between adapting and following one's own path.

The *Warrior* knows what he wants, knows how to get it and goes for it.
The shadow poles *Masochist* and *Sadist* experience power and aggression as an end in itself. They respectively express the intrinsic need to be a victim of duty or violence, or to make victims by any means.

An XIP needs the *Warrior* to effectively channel his natural drive.

Nurturer and Magician

The *Nurturer* and the *Magician* or *Shaman* are concerned with knowledge gained through experience, while dealing with material and immaterial affairs. In Xi terms, this is about skills to deal with complexity.

The *Nurturer* knows how to stimulate growth, and produce a rich harvest. She manages the process of making the right combinations to create something new. She combines knowledge and senses.
The shadow poles *Barren Field* and *Poisoner* prevent a harvest, either by infertility and neglect, or by wickedness and intrigue.
Xi *Nurturers* are blessed with much that can contribute to growth and development and are able to guide complex processes to a successful end.

The *Magician* possesses knowledge in his mind and his body and is fully aware of its connections, as it is between male and female, or form and substance. He combines knowledge and intuition.
The shadow poles *Denier* and *Detached Manipulator* pervert the richness of knowledge by denying it, or by detaching it from its context, leading to faked innocence or evidence.
The *Xi Magician* is a Master of his trade or of his trades. One trade is often not sufficient to fulfil all his creative needs.

Hostess and Lover of life

The *Hostess* and the *Lover of life* are by nature focused on experiencing all that life has to offer and enjoying this to the full.
Expressed in Xi terms, we are talking about dealing with intensity.

The *Hostess* receives people and offers them shelter from the heart. It is her passion to enter into relations with warmth.
The shadow poles *Noncommittal* and *Pushover* are unable to handle their own boundaries in a relationship well, resulting in either blocked, or complete absent ones.
The *Xi Hostess* is a natural centre of joy and consolation, almost like a horn of plenty. The *Xi Hostess* is also relatively vulnerable to finding herself in one

of her shadow poles. Through dealing with being "different from the average," she runs the risk of compensating by being too permissive or disappointedly slamming the door shut.

The *Lover of life* has great vitality. He enjoys everything life brings him and has the propagation of beauty as his goal. He lives his passions but is not a slave to them.
The shadow poles *Depressive* and *Addict* suffer from a lack of enjoyment or an overindulgence in it. Their link between mind and body is distorted: They don't accept their physical existence or are controlled by their physical needs.
The *Xi Lover of life* experiences life thanks to his high sensitivity (and other areas of Xr) with unusual intensity. He creates beauty through elegant ideas, or craftsman like creativity.
As in the case of the Xi-Hostess, the shadow forms of the Xi Lover of life are near. Some XIPs sink under all possible addictions, while others remain depressed in their intensely experienced disappointments.

Director and King

The *Director* and the *King* are concerned with the capacity to find one's place in the world and take it in a clear, self-assured way. The archetypes are about own sovereignty and authority and, expressed in Xi terms, represent the vital merging of intensity, complexity and drive.

The *Director* knows the right moment, the right people and the right rituals to allow events to take place effectively and expressively. She takes undisputed charge of the process and links past, present and future.
The shadow poles, *Absentee* and *Control Freak*, have too little or too much presence: One exerts no influence on events; the other has a stifling influence.
In her driven manner the *Xi Director* gives form to complex and intense processes, leading to unorthodox results being achieved in a way that is meaningful for the participants.

The *King* rules his kingdom well and embodies its sovereignty. He creates order and justice. He offers possibilities for expression and affirms everybody fully in their capacities.

The shadow poles, *Weakling* and *Tyrant*, mishandle order and justice. One by lacking authority to carry it through, the other by perversion of what authority is meant for.

The *Xi King* has taken control of his special talent: Not to dominate but because he cannot do anything other than infuse the world with his quality. It is a quiet power, even though it carries responsibility with it. Thanks to his strong sense of justice, he gives everyone his or her due.

THE DEGREE OF XI

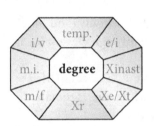

It is easy to imagine that gradations of Xi exist. One person is, for example, structurally more curious than the other, or knows even fewer boundaries. In other words: extra intense, extra complex, and extra driven.

The stronger the extra intelligence is, the more uncommon the XIP is, by definition, and most often, the more important a proper management of this gift of being uncommon will be. In the figure shown, the *degree of Xi* is situated in the heart, because it is our experience that it works as a reinforcing factor for the entire Xidentity. The higher the degree of Xi, the more striking some facets will be, while others are more extensive, or one has to deal with them more carefully to achieve maximum expression.

When identifying the eight facets of the Xidentity, it is relevant to take this ninth facet into account: the possibility of possessing certain characteristics to a stronger or weaker degree than other XIPs in one's environment – in other words – to be uncommon *within* the population of XIPs.

It is a good idea to first quantify just how extreme this uncommonness can be.

Extremely uncommon means difficult to compare

Despite all its limitations, the IQ score is a simple quantitative basis for comparison purposes.

If we compare the statistical figures for IQ = 100 (average), 130 (gifted), 145 (highly gifted) and 160 (exceptionally gifted), then we notice:

- Of every 22 people with an above-average IQ, 1 person is gifted.

- Of every 17 *gifted* individuals, 1 person is highly gifted.
- For every 800 *highly gifted* individuals, 1 person is exceptionally gifted.[12]

If we realize that we know from experience that gifted individuals often feel different in the company of people having average intelligence, then this is exceptionally more so for people with an IQ of over 145. Those highly gifted can even still feel different in the company of "normally" gifted individuals.

In the right diagram of figure 4 in chapter one – shown again here – they do not occur, because their "dot" falls outside the frame of the diagram, meaning that they rarely meet people who are more or less similarly gifted. An important step in the acknowledgement of someone's *extreme* intelligence (i.e. the first Practice) is therefore dealing with and accepting of this extreme uncommonness that has in it characteristics of structural loneliness.

Often the path to expression of Xi (i.e. the third Practice) is a major challenge. Training institutes are not really equipped to deal with extreme learning needs, so they are not always able to assess that need accurately, let alone to stimulate it.
Thinking out of the box, inventing a *new* wheel does not immediately lead to financing, facilities or respect, certainly not if explaining to others what you mean in a clear fashion is by definition a challenge; for the extreme XIP, it can be virtually impossible to put himself/herself in the mindset of the slower thinking of others.

Characteristics of an extreme degree of Xi

With extreme Xi, one can expect communication to occur in a higher gear, the leaps in thought to be bigger... or is there more to it?
There is little literature available on extreme adult giftedness.[13]

---

[12] The figures are derived from the precise nσ value of a normal distribution.
[13] I refer here to American literature where from "highly gifted" (IQ ≥ 145) and above is spoken of extreme giftedness.

The size of the group is very small (0,1%). Also the available data are relatively limited and in the light of chapter one, widely varied.
Based on literature (Powell & Haden, 1984), but also on our own observations, we have established that extreme XIPs indeed go a step further in cognitive ability.
Compared with individuals of average intelligence, XIPs are well able to structure information in a new manner, and therefore to make new relations between areas that were initially separated from each other.
Where averagely intelligent individuals are skilled in analysis, XIPs are also strong in synthesis.

Extreme XIPs are able to *simultaneously* analyse and synthesize. They work with a helicopter view but at the same time watch every move of the ants on the ground. They do not lose themselves in details, and their perception is both global and detailed. This is the result of extremely efficient information processing, which for them takes place automatically. That is why they are perfectly suited to create systems that are founded on new paradigms.
Successful exceptional historic examples are Newton, Einstein and Madame Curie in the sciences. More recent and different examples are Tim Berners-Lee, the inventor of the World Wide Web, Balanchine in ballet, Glass in music, Picasso in the visual arts, or Johan Cruijff in soccer.

The ruthless critic

The most formidable opponents of the effective expression of their excellence can be the extreme XIPs themselves. They apply their superior capacity for information processing to their environment, and pre-eminently to themselves. The speed with which they think things through or think up a new concept is rarely in proportion to the time required for its realization or materialization. So they follow their own actions extraordinarily critically and each aspect of apparent failure is observed faultlessly. The existential question posed by many XIPs: "Am I good enough?" has long been translated as "I'm *never* good enough." The reasons may vary, but not the conclusion.
Sometimes XIPs decide that in future they will leave things at the concept stage, and not continue toward the realization. The underlying conclusion:

"Apparently, I'm not fit for anything, so I'd better make sure that I don't get noticed. On top of that I don't want to be humiliated again."

It is possible that the childhood environment of extreme XIPs contributes to the low level of self-esteem, the Xinasty facet.

For example, parents were constantly concerned, or tried to correct rigorously the extremely "being uncommon" of their child. They were possibly motivated by their own fears as a result of what they themselves had gone through, and wished to protect their child or pupil from the feared bad ending or the pain.

Here, too, children can function as a mirror for their parents, and what parents observe in their children can be a reason to re-assess their own position regarding the subject. It is never too late for that!

Part Three

The third Practice: Applying Xi

Chapter 5 *The Diversity of Applying Xi*

The first Practice, *Acknowledging Xi*, is by no means simple, but is in a way quite straightforward. The issue is relatively clear, although everyone's personal angle on it is different. By consequence it may take relatively little or enormous effort to truly acknowledge being an XIP and enjoying Ximension.

The second Practice, *Exploring Xi*, is a more complex issue because of the different facets of Xidentity and their various aspects. It takes conscious effort to make the investigation and it takes personal courage for an XIP to face the results, both one's personal fragility and one's specific uncommon power.

One might think the third Practice is just the application of the knowledge of the first and second Practice: One acknowledges having extra intelligence, one knows one's particular strengths and weaknesses, let's apply this knowledge and everything will work out fine!

Nevertheless, the third Practice is about *applying* one's *extra intelligence* and that complicates the issue and may decrease expected effectiveness.

CHARTING A COURSE FOR THE THIRD PRACTICE

Many XIPs perform quite easily on a typically good level of operations. They are not challenged to excel or have their own reasons for not wanting to. In fact, they can be quite effective XIPs as long as they are happy with the situation. Some of them though may have hobbies of a quite extraordinary level of complexity or intensity and express the *extra* of their Xi there.

But due to organizational or personal changes, or due to entering a new phase in life, happiness may begin to wane and while searching for a new balance, the innate habit of or need for intensity, complexity, and drive kicks in: "Is that all there is? I was hoping for something different!"

Other XIPs are already eager from the start of their career to contribute to society, and start to work with all guns blazing. But their zeal and proficiency may be threatening to their environment, and their efforts get slowed down or worse. They try a new job, but experience the same frustration quite soon: "Why is my contribution not properly valued?"

Applying Xi is about the process of putting one's *extra* intelligence to effective use in a certain environment or context. It is the most unspecified Practice:

> *It is about stretching your limits, like venturing into new territory with only a sketch for a map.*
> *It is about looking for an unknown connection between two different subjects or disciplines: You know it must exist, and are determined to discover or prove that it does.*
> *Your Xi is not a form of expression that "Everyone can do," rather, you are trying to find the proper use for your specific kind of extra intelligence in a sustainable way.*

There is no standard recipe or procedure for the Practice of Applying Xi, and we see three reasons for this:

1. Due to the inherent diversity of XIPs, their *form* of expression is similarly diverse: Every description of the typical application of Xi has by definition very many variations and exceptions.
2. Applying one's Xi in a certain form is the result of a *process* that takes some time. This process is very specific to the XIP in question.
   Barriers or incentives for sustained action differ widely, depending on the XIP's personal history of acknowledgement of his/her own Xi and his/her Xidentity. A meaningful *general description* of the process of applying Xi is by definition questionable.
3. The application of one's Xi, essentially, is a very *personal experience* that involves awareness of one's senses and a focused state of mind. It is illogical and possibly distracting to suggest a *prescription*, even if this is tempting in a book on management and effective XIPs.

Firstly, I will explain in this Part how differently this can work out given the diversity of XIPs, illustrated through the four temperaments and the typology of "superstars, strivers and independents."

The most complicated theme of the third Practice is about two competing dimensions that always have to be considered in order to develop one's personal effective mix of the two: The balance between *Autonomy* and *Rapport* in the process of applying one's Xi.

Many XIPs need a certain autonomy to be creative. Exchanging gifts creates rapport. Fulfilling expectations of excellent performance creates rapport too, but striving for mastery or personal excellence may need making autonomous decisions that put rapport at risk.

I have the impression that the mentioned diversity of XIPs also implies that different XIPs encounter different aspects of this balance between autonomy and rapport. They are put together in chapter six: *Applying Xi amid the Norm*. Different readers will probably have different recognition and appreciation of the five sections of that chapter.

In our career coaching practice, we have developed various instruments, workshops, training sessions and processes to facilitate XIPs finding their way in the Practices, including the third Practice of applying Xi. Basically this entire book is inspired by our personal experiences, both as being XIPs, and through our experiences of the last 10 years with adult XIPs. In chapter seven and in the Appendix, however, I will make more explicit how its content has developed over the last years through my own personal endeavour to apply *my* Xi. Making explicit how I have been pressing forward to apply my Xi for the last couple of years is not meant to show off, or to prescribe that everyone should follow my path.

Rather it means:

1. To embody a work in progress. Applying Xi is basically about that.
2. To make explicit that it takes time and effort and does not always work out as intended or hoped for. Being an XIP is not a free ride to success.
3. To illustrate that XIPs very often have multiple fields of interest and that they are naturally inclined to search for ways to connect these various fields into a new discipline, as a reflection of how they try to connect this knowledge in their own minds and bodies.
4. To offer a couple of maps that someone may recognize as practical sketches for certain kinds of terrain that are familiar because of earlier ventures into new territory.
5. To create a structure in these chapters on the third Practice that allows both for a conceptual perspective of, and a practical identification with the subject, to obtain maximal effectiveness.

THE DIVERSITY OF EXCELLENCE AND LEADERSHIP

According to the New Oxford American Dictionary, to excel means: *to be exceptionally good at or proficient in an activity or subject.*
That is what one would expect of "uncommonly intelligent people" in the first place. We already explained the diversity of XIPs and the consequences of that characteristic in chapter three.
The aim of the third Practice, applying Xi, is indeed to experience excellence or mastery of the process, and if possible also to reach excellent results. Those results may be very diverse: The theory of multiple intelligences (chapter four) illustrates that in an obvious way; the musician comes to another presentation of excellence than the mathematician or the charismatic leader.

Temperament theory on the other hand, explains how different temperaments may use a variety of approaches to become or be excellent. We outline some characteristics as examples of this variety:

The Artisan will experience his/her excellence while:
  Creating something of special beauty;
  Managing ten activities simultaneously;
  Performing with ultimate craftsmanship;
  Surviving quite considerable risks with grace;
  Leading by taking immediate and effective action.

The Guardian will experience his/her excellence after:
  Realisation of a very adequate organizational structure;
  Restoring an old, venerable tradition;
  Remaining unfalteringly loyal and conscientious;
  Contributing vitally to the continuity of a group;
  Becoming a renowned, competent and trustworthy leader.

The Idealist will experience a feeling of excellence through:
  Bringing harmony to dissonance;
  Overcoming a personal barrier in his/her development;
  Connecting with somebody in a genuine healing way;
  Trusting his/her own intuition fully;
  Leadership in the promotion of peace and justice.

The Rationalist will consider the following as excellent:
The development of a new and comprehensive theory;
The exposure of a theory that is not logically consistent;
The application of ultimate efficiency;
The perfect composure, whatever may happen;
Leadership for conceiving a definitely successful strategy.

Please note the four different perceptions of *true leadership* of those four temperaments:

- Taking immediate and effective action;
- Structuring and managing in a reliable and competent way;
- Inspiring with warmth, good ideas and causes;
- Strategic and efficiency-driven planning;

This is another reason why it is hardly possible to put down a general description of how to apply one's Xi and achieve excellence as an XIP.

Result or process?

Similarly it shows that it may depend on the temperament of the "audience" whether an XIP will get applause or official rewards for his/her excellent achievements. For the Olympic sportsperson it seems straightforward: winning medals, preferably golden ones. For the academic it is similar: counting the number of refereed articles, prestigious awards or scholarships. But is the sportsperson not excellent while training all year long and studying new methods, equipment, schedules?
Are academics not excellent while working on their articles and trying to discover something unknown?
And what about the excellence of extremely diligent and capable managers, secretaries, volunteers, ministers or teachers at all levels and many other professionals, pushing their limits, reinventing their jobs or their professions? Can they consider themselves "excellent appliers of their Xi" only after having received more pay, publicity, or promotion?

For XIPs, the important thing is to be aware of their own process of expression, to know what makes it more effective, to know their own strengths and motivation, to go for it and thoroughly enjoy stretching, growing and expressing themselves to the fullest. This is enlarged upon in chapter six, in the section on performance, mastery and personal leadership.

SUPERSTARS, STRIVERS, INDEPENDENTS

In her book, *Gifted Grownups, The Mixed Blessings of Extraordinary Potential*, American author Marylou Streznewski (1999) broadly divides gifted individuals into three categories: superstars, strivers and independents. She devised these categories after interviewing 100 adults and adolescents who had previously achieved exceptionally high scores on their IQ tests. Her ordering can be used for recognition of XIPs but even more so for describing three different styles for, or circumstances of applying Xi.

The fascinating issue is whether the XIP is somehow aware of being uncommon and of the personal process of expression. If that is not the case, whether would more awareness make a difference and induce choosing another category to increase personal effectiveness?

I have added different forms of the graph that I introduced in chapter one.

Superstars

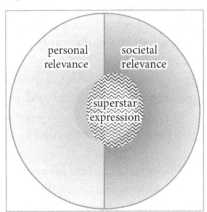

Figure 9: Superstars, exceeding expectations

People expect all gifted individuals to be superstars. The XIPs who can be recognised as superstars are "taller, healthier, handsomer, wealthier, happier, and nicer than most people." (Streznewski, 1999, p.7) They work hard but also play hard: They do a lot of things outside their work: They involve themselves in social activities, sports, culture, etc. They excel in whatever field they operate in. Their values are typically in line with the values of their environment and their lust for life is just as above average as their performance. Figure 9 shows how the actual expression is much larger than the white half-circle of the expected norm for performance. The expression focuses more on societal relevance than personal relevance.

The subject of Xi often holds little interest for superstars because they feel no need to have an explanation for being one. As far as they are concerned, they have always achieved things with little effort on their part.

Strivers

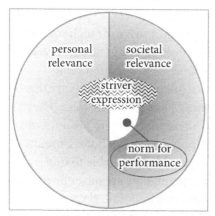

Figure 10: Strivers, married to their work

XIPs who can be recognised as strivers work incredibly hard – at school, at work, in everything they do. They produce almost superhuman performances, all based on their inner motivation. They appreciate structure and clear leadership. They typically do not come up with innovative scientific or cultural results but what they do, they do in an extraordinarily meticulous way and the most appropriate manner. The adults often consider themselves to be married to their work. Figure 10 shows that strivers perform in specific fields and exceed expected performance amply but only locally. Their focus is more on societal relevance than on personal relevance, illustrated by their expression being more on the right half of the circle.

For them, too, Xi is typically not a topic that interests them: They explain their above-average performances as being a result of their above-average desire to work and abundance of energy. They are too concerned with work to be distracted by side issues like wondering about their uncommonness. If strivers enter our career coaching practice, this is often as a result of a temporary lack of motivation, which might, for example, be caused by overstrain, burnout, or the life phase they are in, typified by the question: "Is that all there is?"

Independents

If something grabs the interest of independents, they will work hard at it in a creative and often brilliant manner. They possess a deep-rooted personal value system. They pay no attention to anything that does not interest them, irrespective of the consequences. Because they are the square pegs in the round holes of society, their career path can run rather unpredictably. If there are issues of authority at play, independents can be enormously uncooperative, and conflicts can run high.

They typically attach no value to being popular.

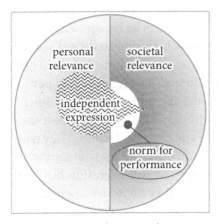

Figure 11: Independents, not fitting in

Figure 11 shows how independents do not fit the norm for performance. They do not strive for high societal relevance either but their expression can have great personal value.

More often, independents are innovators rather than followers. They are the ones most likely to produce the invention that constitutes a breakthrough. If you are able to understand them, they are never boring and always inspirational. If you cannot understand them, they'll drive you crazy.

The social breakthrough of these creative XIPs can take a long time to manifest, if at all. This can result in them abandoning all social links or lead to criminal behaviour and even death.

Independents have much to gain by exploring the topic of Xi, certainly if they have negative experiences with "being different from their environment:" Even though they are the most talented of the three groups, they are often the least understood by their environment.

The acknowledgement of Xi can be the catalyst that leads to "hearing the sound of pennies dropping," so that they are better able to let their talents loose on the world.

Chapter 6 *Applying Xi amid the Norm*

An important aspect in enjoying the gift of being uncommon is dealing with standards and commonness, which are Norms that our society has great affinity with.
In this chapter, I will discuss various aspects of this possible tension that many XIPs have to work out for themselves:

- between a need for autonomy and a need for rapport;
- between a drive for personal mastery and an expected performance;
- between a passion for excellence and the massive stability of the average.

I will also come back to the topic of gift and gifted as introduced in chapter one, and the differences between gift reciprocity and market economy. I will illustrate it with the differences among superstars, strivers and independents. The different sections are not independent of each other; although they consider different perspectives, the issues can be similar.
Again, I do not have prescriptions to offer. I have not added case studies either. But I do hope that explaining the possible tension and the resulting ambiguous prods to choose either of the two options, helps readers to find their own way in their current situation.

AUTONOMY AND RAPPORT, INTERDEPENDENCE
Autonomy is one of the five characteristics of Xi, as stated in the first chapter.

> ***Needs autonomy****: Can work on his/her own and prefers to schedule tasks independently. Will respond aversely to absolute power and formalities, and react allergically to superiors or others who exercise tight control. Will utilize fight or flight response when autonomy is threatened.*

One of the reasons behind this need for autonomy lies in the high level of extra receptivity (Xr) that all XIPs have, which makes them experience life differently and more intensely than normally intelligent people. In combination with their uncommon capacity for information processing, they prefer to be able to follow their own sensory impulses for action. They also prefer to organize their work following their own logic, thereby doing things in a way that makes sense to them and is efficient in their eyes. That is, after all, one of the reasons why they are naturally able to come up with innovations, new theoretical concepts, different approaches to common problems, and so on.

Rapport is the word for a good relationship between people who understand and mostly agree with each other's opinions and ideas.
XIPs usually have mixed experiences with rapport, due to their relatively uncommon qualities, as the earlier introduced figure 4 illustrates. Their opinions and ideas often differ from what majorities think to be right or normal.

Additionally, many XIPs have a strong intuition about what others are thinking. They can be painfully aware whether there is too little rapport, because the other person insufficiently understands or shares their opinions and ideas. XIPs are vividly aware that rapport is not self-evident, as they have excellent memories.

XIPs experience very strongly the human needs for security, social contact, and some form of appreciation and love, due to their extra receptivity or – more generally – their intensity. They will maintain high standards for their own contribution to a relation and will go a long way to live by those standards themselves.

Additionally, to realize one's plans while applying Xi, one often needs the support and agreement of others, so there is also a pragmatic reason for establishing an adequate relation with them, perhaps it is even inevitable.

So here it is: XIPs need their autonomy to be uncommonly creative and to be able to process and evaluate their continuously high sensory input in their own way in order to maintain their mental (and physical) health.
XIPs also need rapport to fulfil their emotional needs and to position their creative actions within their context or environment.
In the case of XIPs, the competition between those two needs is rather fierce, and the outcome may be unstable or change over time.

Technically, the solution is to strive for rapport while maintaining a sufficient level of autonomy, thereby illustrating how we are neither completely dependent nor independent of each other, but interdependent. But XIPs have to find their own optimal mix, depending on various facets of their Xidentity. Two examples to illustrate this:

> *XIPs who are more extra task-oriented (see chapter four) will generally be more attentive to keeping sufficient autonomy, while extra empathics are more focused on maintaining rapport.*
>
> *For very different reasons, Artisans will also place their autonomy higher than rapport, valuing highly their freedom to act, while Idealists may prefer rapport to autonomy, unless this would be a threat to the furthering of authenticity, one of their most important values.*

Benefits through Ximension

We introduced Ximension as the dimension where being Xi goes without saying and as a place to stock up and recharge before expressing oneself in the "normal" world. This makes Ximension a special environment to experiment with one's optimal level of autonomy and rapport. Generally speaking, a pleasant level of rapport between XIPs develops relatively easy in Ximension, almost by itself, which makes it relatively safe to experiment there with more autonomy. This implies allowing oneself to be more daringly creative, while enjoying the intense exchange of sensory input and processing that the interaction among XIPs entails and the natural rapport in Ximension.

This is one of the reasons why it can be very profitable for organizations to allow or stimulate interaction between their XIPs, even when they do not work in the same department, nor are cooperating on a regular basis. They will inspire and support each other to do their own job better, and recharge their batteries at the same time.

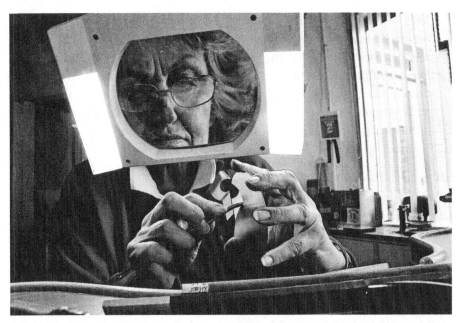

Magda has an eye for detailed work, just like she experiences everything in a detailed way. She has tremendous energy to find out new techniques and to extend her borders in the use of different materials – in this case, silver. She cherishes her autonomy while doing this but also actively organizes rapport by giving courses and sharing her craft with others.

Mariska holds strong views on the necessity of excellent quality for her work as an artist but also for the way she displays the works of fellow artists in her gallery. She is actively aware of her intuition, sensitivity and intensity. While working on a painting she is completely autonomous in this activity. With her courses and the activities in her studio/gallery she creates rapport with her environment and with the town community.

GIFT RECIPROCITY VERSUS MARKET ECONOMY

The importance of autonomy for realizing uncommon creations plus the need for rapport to give context to the creations, can also be viewed from the perspective of *gift-exchange* as introduced in chapter one.

As I explained there: being Xi is a gift, inspiration is a gift, and their products also have a gift-like quality. XIPs can be aware of this and feel the need to make a contribution to society, thereby maintaining the cycle of giving. They may feel reluctant to "sell" their assets for lots of money, like one would sell a scarce commodity. But they may feel vulnerable and even rejected when representatives of society do not show any interest in their products, or belittle them for not being able to produce according to regular standards.

I will first come back to the book, *The Gift*, by Lewis Hyde (2007) and its description of the differences between gift-exchange and market economy and their consequences for the creative artist. After that, the similarity with XIPs and the characteristic differences between superstars, strivers and independents become readily apparent.

Differences between gift-exchange and market economy

Hyde elaborates on how there are considerable differences between a society that is governed by the rules of gift-exchange and one that uses the rules of a market economy for the trading of its commodities.

- Traditionally, gifts are a kind of circulating wealth that establishes and maintains a relation between the giver and the person who accepts the gift.
  Commodities are possessions; their owners decide autonomously whether to sell and for what price.
- Gifts are meant to be consumed, used, or passed on in another form to remain gift-like; commodities are possessions that can be taken out of circulation.
- The value of a gift is not negotiable; the price of a commodity is.
- In a gift society the highest esteem is for the person who gives the most. In a market economy the highest esteem is for the person who takes the most (shown by having accumulated the greatest wealth).

- Usually, a gift-based society defines a boundary between the people who are bounded to that society through their gift-exchanges, and the people who are not. The latter are supposed to pay for certain goods or services, while the first are treated differently. In other words, a gift that passes such a boundary either stops being a gift or abolishes the boundary.
  A commodity can cross the boundary without changing its nature.
  In fact, the commodity-like exchange may establish a boundary where none previously existed.
- Refusing gifts or asking money for rendered services is a way to prevent coming too close to the other.

Artists in the modern world

In Hyde's view, artists in the modern world experience a tension between their creative environment, where art is created in a gift atmosphere, and their market environment, where their work generates their income.
For practical reasons, a part of the gift-exchange between artist and buyer occurs through the buyer giving money to the artist. But still artists may feel reluctant to sell – read *partly give* – their work of art to someone dislikeable, or feel inclined to raise its price considerably for compensation.
Many artists engage an agent for the market environment to be able to concentrate on creating in the gift environment. Some artists are given a form of patronage or grants, so that they do not have to worry about how to deal with the market. Other artists just do not manage to find an effective agent or a patron, because of the unconventional, unexpected or unwanted qualities of their art. Quite a number of artists have a job for a limited amount of time to earn enough money for daily costs, while using their free time for the expression of their true gifts. In most cases artists acquire little material wealth during their lives and in many cases are not bothered too much by this situation: Their mind is set on the expression of their gifts and the cycle of giving.
As Hyde points out:

> ...There are categories of human enterprise that are not well organized or supported by market forces. Family life, religious life, public service, pure science, and of course much artistic practice...any community that values these things will find nonmarket ways to organize them. It will develop gift-exchange institutions dedicated to their support. (p. 370)

He is intrigued by the processes that lead to the forming of those institutions that support non-commercial enterprises. He is aware that they will inevitably change over time, along with the perceived value of those enterprises.

XIPs in the modern world

In my view, XIPs may experience a tension similar to that of the mentioned artists. When they feel this drive to use and share their gift, they may encounter resistance or even rejection from their environment. Will they be able to ask for sufficient payment for their products and services to pay their bills? Will they get the payment they ask for, or have to fight for it?
After all, a gift stops being a gift when its value has to be negotiated. Similarly, rejection of the gift feels like being thrown out of a community. Suddenly it does not feel very nice to acknowledge one's gift and apply it. Perhaps there is no real gift, after all. Perhaps one's inspiration was just an ill wind that brings no good. These kinds of experiences may lead to stagnation and denial of one's Xidentity if they are not properly recognized and managed.

Traditionally, for Xi scientists this possible tension was solved through publicly or privately financed research institutions, formerly called ivory towers. They had extensive freedom to research any subject that was interesting to them and exchange their information freely with other scientists. Many scientists nowadays need to devote part of their time to applied science to earn their income, while using their spare time for fundamental research if they have that drive. They may encounter restrictions in exchanging information freely, due to company or academic journal regulations. The market economy has more influence on their work than before and the prod to perform as expected may lead to stress and diminished creativity.

But what about the XIPs who are not scientists? Do they manage to live simultaneously in the realm of gift reciprocity and market economy? Are they able to find some kind of patronage?
Some of our clients are carefully sent by their managers. Typically these managers explicitly want to talk to us about their feeling that this potential client has special qualities that can be of great value to the organization and that he/she is insufficiently valued at that moment. They consider our coaching to be partly a commercial investment but also a gift to a human being

they value and respect for his/her uncommon contributions to the organization: a reciprocal gift, after all.
Like the artists, some XIPs choose a regular part-time job to earn enough money to be able to be creative in their own way during the rest of the week: They live part-time in each of the two worlds.
Others are too shy or gift-orientedly preoccupied to ask for the money they really deserve after solving complicated problems or creating uncommon solutions or performances. That is where an agent or a temporary employment company may be practical. The medical professionals have solved this by collectively established fees for services. Market economy inspired standard "production times" may hamper their professional urge for mastery in patient care and diminish their motivation and satisfaction.
Let us, by the way, not forget to mention the XIPs who have a special interest in and gift for topics that involve money and its transactions. They may become quite wealthy, just by abundantly applying their gift to the market economy.

A more general description can be made through the in the previous chapter introduced categories of superstars, strivers and independents. All three experience the tension between gift-exchange and market economy very differently.

The *superstars* experience little tension. They obtain high levels of achievement, and although they may consider their own successes as somehow bestowed on them as they are just playing with their possibilities, they play with fervour. They give abundantly and these gifts are returned through public recognition, power and earnings.
As I mentioned already, superstars fit most closely the somewhat romantic image that is usually associated with gifted people. It is a fascinating thought that by coupling the notion of giftedness to performance, the traditional appreciation of a gift-exchange–based community is followed: Adults are only called gifted when and as long as they give abundantly. We do love our superstars (as long as they entertain us with their gifts)!

The *strivers* are a different kind, because they consider themselves successful due to their very hard work, not through the bestowal of gifts at birth, nor through uncontrollable moments of inspiration. They are very motivated of course, and productive, but not necessarily uncommonly creative. As is often said, they seem to be married to their work. Strivers will experience little tension, as they do not feel the need to take part in a gift-exchange. They may refer to their results as 99% perspiration, 1% luck and will consequently feel at ease to ask a good price for their efforts.

The *independents* are most liable to experience this tension, especially when their market environment does not value their creativity or insights properly. To add to this, they experience that their gifts are not accepted, which creates a boundary between them and their environment. Often this may lead to stagnation of their creativity: If the result of effort and creativity is not valued, one becomes critical of one's own inspiration, which usually upsets its occurrence.

Of course, there are independents who manage to come up with something that society values, sometimes after a long struggle, sometimes because they were far ahead of their time.

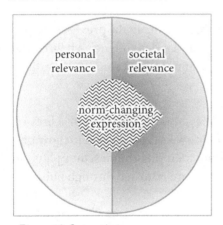

Figure 12: Super pioneers: Changing expectations

One might call them *super pioneers*: They have lots of rapport with society, but somehow manage to keep their autonomy as well.

They keep coming up with new uncommon ideas, refuse to wear conventional clothes and often refer publicly to the importance of respecting one's source of inspiration. They manage to change society's expectations of performance to fit their own excellent expression. Figure 12 illustrates how the super pioneer's expression has changed the shape of the norm for performance. Compared to the superstar, expression has also considerable personal relevance.

An example of realizing the right ideas in the right way at the right moment.

In chapter one I referred to the hypothesis that:
"The less one considers one's Xi to be something special, the easier it is to ask for and accept payments like one does for a commodity."

It is my impression that superstars and strivers are not considering their intelligence as something special, which may explain why they often seem to acquire wealth more easily that independents.
It is a fascinating trend that very wealthy people who earned their money on the market are starting to give away part of their fortune to various funds and goals that they consider valuable for society. Simultaneously, many governments cut on subsidies and other forms of public expenditures due to their high deficits. Together this may lead to new forms of gift-exchange between XIPs and their environment.

In conclusion, some XIPs may find the topic of gift reciprocity versus market economy more relevant than others.
Since many XIPs (and most certainly the independent ones) choose to begin their own enterprise, it is relevant that they are aware of the differences between the trade of gifts and of commodities. Many professionals are naturally proud to be able to express and share their gifts as they like, without company regulations. Where do they want the boundaries of their domain of gift-exchange and expected reciprocity to be? Is their environment of the same opinion? What kinds of services need to be paid for by whom and how is this mutual relation valued by both parties. How does one deal with gifts that are refused or not (sufficiently) reciprocated by customers or clients? How can sufficient funds be obtained without personal embarrassment for supposed rapacity? How is one's self-confidence affected when bills are not paid or the value of the product or service questioned?

PERFORMANCE AND THE PERSONAL CHALLENGE FOR MASTERY

Although having an unusual drive is part of the profile of XIPs, this drive should be underlain with motivation of some kind. In fact, if an XIP is not motivated to do something, the innate drive turns against him/her and results in a depressing feeling of inadequacy and meaninglessness.
According to educational, as well as management theories, motivation can be boosted by setting a goal of some kind. One of the choices that have to be made is whether to choose a performance goal or a mastery goal.
A *performance goal* is about obtaining some well-defined result, like grades at school or production targets at work.

A *mastery goal* is about becoming proficient – a master – in the process of learning or working.

XIPs and their environment have to be aware of the difference between the two, and of the fact that the management of motivation is an important factor in attaining and maintaining effectiveness of XIPs.

The inevitable prod to perform

For many people, having an uncommonly high intelligence means having an obligation to perform in accordance with this "special gift." This is not something to take lightly: In many countries the various special programs for gifted children are of course meant to facilitate them in applying their special intelligence. But "performance" as a driving factor comes along with the special focus on school grades and quite often on blaming when they fall below expectations.

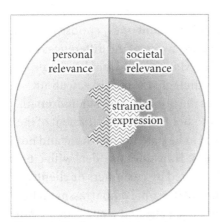

Figure 13: Performance orientation may influence autonomy

Figure 13 shows how the actual expression does cover the white half-circled norm for performance. The personal relevance of the expression, however, seems to be partly missing. Parents can be quite stress-producing too, especially when their children have to fulfil dreams that they themselves could not make into reality. We addressed this in the section on Xinasty in chapter four.

Similarly, the important aim for gifted programs is the "cure for cancer" argument: Teaching gifted children to use their talents will lead to benefits for society because they will make important discoveries in science that will improve the life and status of the country's citizens (and their government).

In her books, *Smart Girls,* and, *Smart Boys,* Barbara Kerr (1994; 2001) tells poignant stories about the atmosphere of special schools and what happened afterwards with the students, their lives and their performance. Although this line of thought – the fulfilment of expectations, and consequent steering onto high performance – is quite logical and from the viewpoint of society understandable, we have our doubts about its effectiveness.

In our experience, many extra empathic XIPs become distracted and develop a fear of failure due to their strong awareness of the expectations of their school or work environment and their loved ones.
They sincerely try to fulfil those expectations. In their endeavour they are less aware of, or forget to address their own needs and to use the qualities they actually have, due to their strong ability to see themselves and their qualities through the eyes of somebody else.
As a consequence, they may fail to perform well on the task at hand, and tend to concentrate even more on the other person and his/her expectations next time, with similar results. And so on.

Task-oriented XIPs are physically less aware of other people's expectations, and may accept a task that is assigned to them and go for it. But, similarly, when the task they undertake matches their own autonomous preferences and qualities, they may be more effective and reach a higher performance.

For the record, one of the obvious complications of adhering to expected performances of XIPs is in the field of innovation and ground-breaking research: Linking the availability of funds to a desired outcome allows little margin to discover something unexpected.

The personal challenge of striving for mastery

The word "mastery" is associated with the medieval guilds, where apprentices had to work and study a long time with their chosen master. Finally, they would produce their own "masterpiece" in order to be accepted in the guild as a master craftsman. This masterpiece was at the least the indication of a high quality of skills and workmanship but also expressed the creative identity of the maker.

Striving for mastery is a strong intrinsic motivation to become proficient to the best of one's abilities. It is about stretching one's limits every time, if possible. It is also connected with personal identity, just as the artist puts his/her name, or rather, personal sign or signature on a finished painting.
"I created this, it is like a part of me."

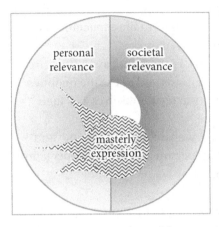

Figure 14: Mastery, unexpected forms of proficiency

In figure 14 this is illustrated by the shape and position of the actual expression: It is certainly up to standards (half circle in the societal relevance part) but somehow in an unexpected, shifted way. The expression in the personal relevance part is firmly rooted.

While striving to make a masterpiece, it is sometimes part of the process to make mistakes while trying a new, possibly better way of doing things, or while finding out one's own individual style of expression.

A mastery orientation helps to try out new ways of learning, or to seek help and inspiration from other masters or even apprentices, because everyone can be a source of knowledge. In the same vein, difficult tasks are usually more fascinating, because there can be something new to master. Perseverance and effort are almost self-evident, because the stretching of personal limits by definition does not come cheap.

IS IT EXCELLENCE OR DEVIANCE?

One of the challenging paradoxes for XIPs is that organizations suggest that they favour excellence but most often react rather against its manifestation. In his captivating book, *Deep Change: Discovering the Leader Within,* American professor Robert E. Quinn (1996) introduces the story of a CEO of a small company that had been acquired by a very large corporation. The small company's unique practices were the secret of its high performance, and the CEO has taken bold actions to prevent the staff of the larger company from instigating processes that would routinize their innovative practices (chapter 19). Quinn has named the chapter "Excellence Is a Form of Deviance" and explains quite simply:

> "Excellence, by definition, requires continued deviance from the norm. When an individual or organization excels, it will encounter pressure to return to conventional behaviour." (p.174)

What makes people in those circumstances persevere in their practice of striving for excellence even if it is without a doubt risky and painful to do so, due to all kinds of resistance or obstructions?
Again Quinn is very direct in his assessment:

> *"We need to recognize that external punishment is a natural process that is never going to end. It forces us to weigh the trade-offs between internal satisfaction and external punishment."* (p. 176)

And he concludes that this reflection usually leads to the feeling that persevering is the right choice to make.
Of course, the history books are filled with examples of uncommonly persevering people who "changed the world." And of course, only the persevering people who *did* change the world enter those books, not the many who were considered obstinate, totally wrong, a nuisance, or were given other unflattering qualifications.

From the perspective of gift-exchange, reciprocation by external punishment is an unconvincing way to promote mutual relations. Gift-exchange driven XIPs must derive their internal satisfaction from a different source than tokens of gratitude from their environment. That is where innate *intensity* and *drive* come in handy and also where a reference to Dabrowski's theory of positive disintegration (see chapter four) can be made. When an XIP feels something is the right thing to do, abstaining is often experienced as far worse than facing the external pressure and criticisms.
Therefore the XIP may persevere in striving for innovative mastery, even under the prod to perform in a more conventional way. By offering the reflection on this process in my book, I hope XIPs and their environment will better understand what is going on and find ways to manage their own situation more effectively.

THE NEED FOR PERSONAL LEADERSHIP

Given the various characteristics of XIPs, like their incurable inquisitiveness, their need for autonomy, their intensity and complexity or their extra receptivity, striving for mastery seems by far to be the most "natural" goal orienta-

tion for them. We already explained the pitfalls of performance orientation in the context of giftedness and XIPs.
The choice seems simple: To maximize effectiveness, go for mastery and refuse to be hemmed in by performance goals.

But the pressure to perform from the environment is not to be underestimated. This can be very easily made visible through the world of sports: Olympic athletes have passed various prior selection processes before being chosen. They are masters in their sports, for example one of the sixteen fastest runners of the world. But for many spectators, or national governments, it's the medal that counts. Ideally, one may read in the papers, "she improved her personal record," but mostly, "he ended not with the first ten" and "she failed expectations."
It seems similar to the topic of *Extra intelligent or Superhuman?* If gaining a Nobel Prize is the only thing that counts, one is unsuccessful and unhappy as long as this has not yet happened. In fact, one should probably work harder or be more creative, on command, mind you!

If the XIP is in need of rapport and appreciation from his/her environment, it is very tempting to go for performance goals: Once you have reached them, you are the hero. The reason can be just as simple as the wish to make Mom and Dad proud, to thank them for all they have done for you.
But the price can be very high: A loss of motivation, energy and self-esteem can occur when the goals are not met. Given the high sensitivity of many XIPs, physical illnesses are not uncommon after proclaimed or even silent failure. After all, there was a lot at stake.

That is why personal leadership is an important quality for XIPs to develop. This involves being clear to oneself about one's choices, dealing with pressure from the environment, and keeping an eye on the personal target, while still being aware of possible interesting information that might influence the goal. Not being too harsh on oneself can also be an important rule.
Of course these issues are important for everyone.
But given the XIP's "extras," his/her system is more easily destabilized, with more consequences. Compare the impact of choices while driving a Formula 1 car, to driving a regular car or riding a bicycle in a small town.
There is a difference and it is wise to take this difference seriously.

Chapter 7   *Tools to Support the Process*

This chapter offers a collection of theories and practical suggestions to help enable the process of applying Xi, the third Practice. Three sections deal with specific subjects that have attracted my interest through books that I have come across. The fourth is a result of many years of interest in chakras and labyrinths.

Given my fascination with the nature and application of Xi, I am always glad to find books that offer a perspective on the nature of interaction and cognition that can be applied especially to XIPs. Awareness of such a perspective may positively influence their effectiveness in applying their Xi.

> *I read some articles about Mirror Neurons in 2008 and found the book of Iacoboni (2008) early 2009. As an empathic I was thrilled by the new perspective about learning and about the physical impact of personal interactions. It led to buying the book on Embodied Cognition by Lakoff and Johnson (1999), the two authors that had also inspired me twenty years earlier with their book, "Metaphors we live by." Both books claim that their subject offers a shift of perspective on centuries of theories about human thinking. As someone with strong independent characteristics (see chapter five) that was immediately attractive and interesting. After many more articles and my own reflections, I am still convinced that it is indeed fascinating.*

There is a rapidly growing body of literature on both embodied cognition and mirror neurons. To my current knowledge, there are no formal research findings in those fields about qualitative or quantitative differences between normal intelligent people and XIPs. In the middle two sections I will briefly outline both subjects, referring mainly to the previously mentioned books and then introduce my own reflections for possible consequences of the theory. These suggestions may help in understanding the various pitfalls and possibilities that influence XIPs in the process of the application of their extra intelligence.

But first I will address the subject of *Mindset* (Dweck, 2006).

MINDSET: PHRASE COMPLIMENTS CAREFULLY

How does it feel when people tell you how fortunate you are with your uncommonly high intelligence and your ease in accomplishing anything?
Do you take your own mistakes very seriously?
Do you think your own intelligence is more or less immutable, or do you think it can be changed by focused effort?

Carol Dweck (2006) has been studying for more than twenty years how our *mindset* creates our world, shapes our goals, and influences our abilities to realize our intentions. There is some similarity with the previous subject of mastery versus performance, but mindset takes a different angle and brings new insights to interaction and thoughts about having uncommon intelligence.
She discerns two basic mindsets:

When you *have a fixed mindset*, you consider your own intelligence and skills steady as a rock, i.e., unchangeable. After all, some people have it, others don't. Therefore it is important to prove time and again that you *do* have it, and behave accordingly at all costs, especially for teachers, managers, customers, colleagues and friends. This brings you success and proves you are indeed a special person.
Because you are smart, everything comes easy for you.
Actually, you don't have to make serious efforts to reach your goals. You believe that it is a proven fact that the owner of real talent wins the race and creates the masterpiece.

When you *practice a growth mindset*, you view intelligence and skills as something that can be developed through focused attention and effort. Being successful has to do with pushing your limits and growing by meeting challenges. You work hardest for the things that really matter to you: In that way you can transform your intelligence and skills. Teachers, managers, customers, colleagues and friends are allies and sources of inspiration on how to learn and transform yourself.
Winning, or being the best is not your main issue, but the process of going all out and enjoying it is.

As long as everything goes smoothly and well, it does not matter that much which mindset one adheres to. But when the going gets tough, or when mistakes are being made, the differences can be extreme.

With a *fixed mindset*, mistakes are a shame, and having to make a real effort for something is a threat to your self-esteem. It evokes the question whether you are that intelligent and special as you (and your environment) were expecting. And since your intelligence is unchangeable, every blemish is a permanent stain. That is why damage control is your first priority: Is there someone else to blame? Will immediate retreat pass unnoticed? Can the results be cunningly improved?
But even when no one has noticed, inside you retain disappointment, shame, and diminished confidence because of this unmistakable sign of personal deficiency.

With a *growth mindset*, mistakes are an invitation to try again differently. Blaming someone is in no way an issue: You cannot make an omelette without breaking eggs. But of course you try to undo the damage and learn how to prevent it the next time.
If the going gets tough, excitement and perseverance step up. Making an effort is invigorating: Now we have a real challenge in order to find out something special!

Although this presentation of the two mindsets makes it quite attractive to try to use the growth mindset, in real life people often have a fixed mindset and even manage to induce others to switch to fixed mindset mode. Just giving them a certain kind of praise or compliments about their high intelligence does the trick, as Dweck time and again has demonstrated in all kinds of situations with all kinds of people very convincingly.
I will paraphrase one of her stories:

> Halfway during some capacity test, one part of the group was praised for their obvious high intelligence, since that had led them to good results so far. Another part of the group was praised for their obvious hard work, that had led those others (also) to good results.
> Then without the groups knowing it, the level of the test became much higher.

> *The members of the group that was praised for their intelligence rapidly gave up or tried to cheat and protested about unfavourable and unfair circumstances, etcetera.*
>
> *The members of the other group, who were praised for their working so hard, started to work even harder, obtained good results, while at the same time visibly enjoying themselves; some were even asking for more questions because they found them really exciting!*

Because the fixed mindset induces the idea that "smart people do not have to work hard or make mistakes," the first group who was told that they were very smart, could not cope with the "humiliating moment of truth" that, after all, they could not be very smart because they had to make a real effort to continue the test.

The second group was stimulated by the increased difficulty to step up their efforts and enjoyed the extra challenge.

What leads to a fixed mindset?

Many XIPs have often experienced being praised extensively for their marked high intelligence. They also were congratulated for their capability of obtaining very high scores at school, practically without effort. For some of them, their obtained high IQ score felt comparable to a graduation in being uncommonly intelligent, plus the irrevocable obligation to behave accordingly.

Fear of failure, apparent laziness, and not persevering under difficult circumstances, are well known complaints about the "underperforming" gifted. Could it be that this typical fixed mindset behaviour is for those children a natural reaction to being praised and labelled as gifted? Can a child have a low or a high susceptibility to this kind of praise? Could this also be the reason why so many adults and children alike resent being denoted gifted, because they somehow feel induced to taking up a fixed mindset, limiting their freedom to make mistakes or fail at a complicated task?

Dweck argues that a fixed mindset is heavily influenced by the kind of compliments that parents and teachers give to children. She extensively researched this and did find out that children indeed like to be praised for intelligence and talent but that it works like a boost with an increased vulnerability for an energy low afterwards.

If you praise children or adults for their efforts instead, it is a completely different story. They like that too and it does not backfire afterwards.

Although the persistency of a fixed mindset is certainly influenced by the wrong kind of praise, it still leaves the question as to why people are so persistent in doing it. Dweck does not seem to acknowledge that there are any advantages to a fixed mindset.
I think that an explanation may be found in the competing values theory of Robert E. Quinn (Cameron and Quinn, 2006). He explains how the need for control and the need for flexibility compete when people want to organize things. Control is usually established by defining preferred stable situations, while flexibility can more easily be described in terms of movement than of stability.
I assume that people who have a strong need for control will more easily make statements like "you are so-and-so," or will like to think that situations are unchangeable: elements of a *fixed* mindset.
People who have a strong need for flexibility will more easily express situational remarks, like "you worked hard for this task, my compliments," and prefer not to be pinned down in permanent qualifications: elements of a *growth* mindset, allowing that things may change.

If my assumption is correct, we may expect that there will always be people who prefer to describe their world in stable concepts. This has advantages and pitfalls, especially in the context of XIPs. After all, we have the strong impression that many qualities of XIPs, especially their capacity to envisage changes, thrive when operating in a growth mindset. On the other hand, their capacity for a comprehensive overview of situations comes in handy when organizations have to be controlled to obtain maximum production or stability: Something a fixed mindset is naturally focused on.

In both cases, it is very relevant for XIPs and their environment to be aware of the effects that compliments and praise about the XIPs' intelligence have on them. When compared to praise about some special effort they have made, it is far less effective. I expect, however, that one XIP may be more susceptible to it than another. Let us definitely try to avoid having a well-meant compliment backfire without being aware of it.

EMBODIED COGNITION (EC)

In their book, *Philosophy in the Flesh, the Embodied Mind and its Challenge to Western Thought*, Lakoff and Johnson (1999) attack head-on the "more than two millennia of a priori philosophical speculation about ... reason." (p. 3)

They refer to empirical discoveries, made possible by the current techniques of neuroscience, which are inconsistent with central parts of Western philosophy about our mind and our ability to rationalize. I list a couple of their initial statements (p. 4):

> *"Reason is not, in any way, a transcendent feature of the universe or of disembodied mind. Instead, it is shaped crucially by the peculiarities of our human bodies, by the remarkable details of neural structure of our brains, and by the specifics or our everyday functioning in the world."*
> *"Reason is evolutionary... Reason, even in its most abstract form, makes use of, rather than transcends, our animal nature."*
> *"Reason is not purely literal, but largely metaphorical and imaginative."*

Descartes' statement: "Cogito, ergo sum," *I think, therefore I am*, can be paraphrased into an embodied cognition (EC) proponent's statement: "Ago, ergo cogito," *I act, therefore I think*. Our moving and our thinking interfere strongly with each other. What is going on in the interaction of our body with our environment will influence what is going on in our brain. People with different types of motor experiences will think in different ways. Understanding is faster and better when students are asked to move or make gestures that correspond to the statement under consideration – this will also be addressed in the next section on mirror neurons. If we consider the proposition that reason makes use of our animal nature, then it is self-evident that we learned while moving to find food and preclude being food. Sitting in classrooms while hardly being allowed to move has introduced a discontinuity in the evolution of our way of learning.

Lakoff and Johnson are champions of the view that the way we make judgments comes from sensorimotor domains. This applies both to abstract things like importance and similarity and to the way we subjectively experience desire, intimacy and achievement. That is why our language is rich in metaphors that are linked to sensorimotor experiences. Their books list beautiful examples to make this clear:

- *"They greeted me warmly."* : Affection is warmth, like being held close.
- *"She's weighed down by responsibilities."* : Difficulties are burdens causing discomfort or disablement, like the carrying of heavy objects.
- *"John's IQ goes way beyond Bill's"* : Linear scales are paths; higher on the scale correlates to visual observation of more progress on a path.
- *"Time flies."* : Time is experienced through observed or performed motion.
- *"She will be successful, but isn't there yet"* : Purposes are destinations like: *"If you want a drink, go to the refrigerator and get it."*

But they go further, relating complex concepts like mind, self, and morality to metaphors based on sensorimotor experiences. It proves the embodiment of reason that major forms of rational inference are instances of sensorimotor inference.
That is why their ultimate point is that philosophy needs to start a dialogue with cognitive science, needs to engage with the best empirical science available. This should prevent philosophy from being just a kind of fabrication of narratives ungrounded in the realities of human embodiment and cognition.

I have expounded on Lakoff and Johnson's books, but there are many interesting sources on embodied cognition to be found in other books, magazines and on the Internet.

Possible applications of the EC concept for XIPs

Assuming that our cognition is embodied makes it easier to understand and accept the often very physical nature of the XIP's intensity and drive. The same applies to their Psychomotor, Sensual and Emotional Extra Receptivity (see chapter four). That is compared to a Cartesian viewpoint of "very clever thinking beings." In fact, from a Cartesian viewpoint, the preference for an IQ score-related approach to the subject is understandable. Our approach through multiple intelligences and the other aspects of Xidentity underlines the relevance of taking more *extra* personal characteristics into full account. These characteristics have much to do with the embodiment of the XIP's mind.

> I have always been intrigued by the differences in status between formal scientific knowledge and experientially acquired knowledge. I find it especially intriguing how scientific knowledge has changed drastically over the decades, sometimes finally acknowledging long standing experiential knowledge without "blushing." (Of course experiential knowledge has also been proven false over time on various occasions.) EC suggests that scientific knowledge is influenced by the special embodiment of the mind of scientists, and that the scientific method does not lead to the discovery of transcendent truths. It is just a different way of thinking.

To make this more precise, suppose a scientific career is relatively facilitated by a strong preference for verbal-linguistic and logical-mathematical intelligences (IQ score boosters), combined with task-orientation and a relatively low degree of emotional and sensual extra receptivity. Following the ideas of EC this embodiment would result in a very specific way of thinking and reasoning, compared to the ways of a person with strong interpersonal and bodily-kinaesthetic intelligences, empathic, with strong psychomotor and emotional extra receptivity. These differences are of course very recognizable in daily practice. But the important issue of EC is that one way of reasoning has no inherent superiority or transcendent truthfulness compared to the other. Traditionally, however, we assume and most often formally establish that the scientific method has this superiority.

I suppose Cartesian thinking fulfils some need or function, otherwise it would not have been so attractive to use it for so long. But let us stop assuming that it is a *superior* way of thinking and let us be aware of its limitations.

Applying Xi is far more effective when consciously embodied. That is, while being consciously aware of one's specific kind of extra receptivity, and other bodily needs and strengths.

Consider for example a preferred learning style:

If one's learning style is relatively *visual*, it is not nice to work in the visually nondescript or even ugly environment some offices excel in. It is like trying to fill a bucket that has a hole in it: The uglier the environment, the larger the hole, and the more effort it takes to fill the bucket.

If one's learning style is relatively *kinaesthetic* – that is learning through moving and experiencing – it is important to walk around in one's office regularly. One should certainly find ways to avoid being forced to sit still during a two-hour meeting, as this results in very low personal effectiveness.

Of course this applies to all people with that kind of learning preference, but with XIPs the disturbing sensory input is more intensely experienced and the negative influence amplified. That is why it deserves extra attention.

In a similar way, one may assume that both the process of mastery – the "path" to excellence – and the metaphor of the labyrinth (see the Appendix) have the attractive association of moving while learning.
Compared to an obligation to perform, or to fit a static mental image of expectations, this may be another explanation for the difference in effectiveness between setting goals for mastery or for performance.

MIRROR NEURONS (MNs)

In 1996 the first article by Vittorio Gallese et al. appeared on the intriguing results in their laboratory at the University of Parma in Italy. They had discovered a special class of neurons in the monkey brain that did not only fire when an individual performs a simple goal-directed action, like picking a piece of fruit, but also when that individual *sees someone else* picking fruit. These new neurons were given the name of Mirror Neurons (MNs) because they "reflected" someone else's action in the owner's brain.
Various empirical findings, and the possibilities of modern non-invasive brain-scanning techniques, have led to a surge in interest and all kinds of research about these MNs and their characteristics.

Vilayanur Ramachandran, one of the prominent researchers, made the often-cited quote: "Mirror neurons will do for psychology what DNA did for biology." In other words, the knowledge about MNs will have the effect of a considerable shift in thinking about various cognitive processes and their impact on human interaction. Ramachandran has found that people with autism show a lack of MN activity in several regions of the brain. This means that they physically experience other people's actions in a different way than more empathic people do.
Other findings (Iacoboni, 2008) show the enormous importance of MNs in learning and influencing in general. MNs help us to perceive intentions of other people's actions: We simulate their actions (mostly without our own physical movement) and become aware of what this action does to us.

We imitate other people's facial expression and through this imitation feel what the other person feels.

> *In a fascinating experiment people are asked to assess the emotional state of other persons by looking at their photographs. This leads to certain numbers of correct and non-correct answers, depending on empathic qualities. Next the same persons are asked to put a pencil squarely between their teeth, impeding the movement of (the corners of) their mouth, and to assess similar photographs. The number of correct answers drops significantly: The personal facial expression is limited, also limiting the physical imitation of the others' facial expression.*
> *Similarly it is found that empathic people have more facial flexibility than people with autism-related characteristics. Empathics are able to imitate more possible emotional states with their facial muscles, thereby experiencing the other's emotions more accurately.*

MNs appear to be multimodal: Hearing the *sound* of someone else cracking peanuts, activates the brain area involved with the action of cracking peanuts just as *looking* at someone else doing it does.

Another discovery is about physical imitation: If one stands in front of someone else and is asked to imitate gestures, there are two ways one can imitate: either mirror-wise (if you raise your left arm, the other raises his/her right arm) or anatomically correct (if you raise your left arm, the other also raises the left arm). Children will until the age of 10-12 always imitate mirror-wise. When adults are asked, mirror-wise imitation is executed slightly faster than anatomically correct imitation. These facts correlate with findings that MNs react about four times more strongly with mirror-wise imitations, compared to anatomically correct ones.

A stronger preference to mirror-wise imitation seems to be connected to a relatively stronger physical intimacy between two people.

There appears to be a strong connection between gestures and the development and understanding of language. There are experiments where people simultaneously gesture and talk that show that they make the correct gesture before they find or express the right word.

MNs are extra active when the telling of a story is accompanied by *iconic* gestures: a gesture that supports the spoken word through a visual image. The story is understood better and faster.
Similarly, understanding is considerably hampered when the spoken words do not match the gestures that are made simultaneously.

Possible applications of the concept of MNs for XIPs

The experimental findings about mirror neurons explain in a completely new way why and how XIPs are heavily and bodily influenced by the behaviour of their environment. Let us assume that XIPs have more and/or more diversely connected MNs than normal intelligent people, similar to other aspects of their neurological make-up. This makes it easier to understand why and how many XIPs are *extra* empathic, or why all XIPs have uncommon fast and diverse ways of learning, even while very young.

There seems to be a difference between MNs for cognitive tasks and MNs for relational information. People with autism have relatively few MNs for the latter. Given the similarity between *extra* extra task-orientation and autistic behaviour, I assume that task-oriented people also have relatively fewer MNs for relational information. That does not, however, impede their abilities for cognitive learning and tasks. I do not know whether they have relatively more MNs for cognitive tasks to compensate.

MNs are more active when other people's activities fit in with a context that is also familiar to us: We perceive intentions. Imaginal thinking is more involved with context than verbal thinking: Images stimulate all kinds of associations, and these associations are most often embodied, because they are connected to sensory inputs. It is no wonder then, that strong imaginal thinkers often easily understand each other without the need to finish their sentences. Something that can be quite unsettling to their environment, by the way.

We have noted that both imaginal thinkers and empathics have a high ability for perspective taking: adopting the perspective or point of view of someone else. Their score on Davis' Interpersonal Reactivity Index is much higher than that of relatively task-oriented people. It is most likely that MNs are crucial to the ability of perspective taking.

Given the plasticity of the brain, and the uncommon complexity and learning capacity of the brain of XIPs, it is plausible that they are able to increase their MN capacity relatively fast by practice and focused use.
This might be an explanation for a well-known phenomenon of gifted children: They are often inclined to take responsibility for emotional burdens of their parent(s) to support them. This heavy load impedes their own development, but they cannot easily stop doing this.
When other people's emotional pain is so physically present in your own body through your MNs, it cannot really be ignored. Additionally, it may be difficult to learn to differentiate between your own pain and the pain that you are aware of through your MNs.

Given the natural "limitlessness" of XIPs, it is of the utmost importance for *empathic* XIPs to become bodily aware of the necessity of a boundary between themselves and the other person. Similarly it is important to pay attention to the daily maintenance of this boundary: There is a limit to the amount of other people's worries one can carry along while keeping good health and vitality. Understanding how their MNs physically force empathics to empathize may help to convey how urgent it is to pay conscious attention to this issue.

MNs make us move along with the general movement around us. When their environment strongly propounds prejudices such as supposed intellectual or performance inferiority of women, the relatively empathic female XIPs are more easily influenced than the task-oriented ones. S. Baron-Cohen (2003) has found characteristic patterns of male systemizing versus female empathising. It has more recently been established that women have statistically stronger MN activity than men. Both results make the impact and persistence of various gender issues more understandable.
Let us try to accept that differences in embodied cognition do not imply superiority or inferiority and be open to letting variety create value.

A MAP OF STAGNATION AND FLOWING EXPRESSION

As discussed in chapter five, there is no universal recipe for the Practice of applying Xi. I have explained various influencing aspects, both from a theoretical point of view and based on our personal experience.

In this section I will summarize the results of my research on the relevance and use of *chakra theory* and the *labyrinth pattern* for designing two tentative maps of the process of expression for XIPs:

- One map to illustrate various reasons for stagnation of the expression;
- One map to depict an effectively flowing expression.

These maps can be used for inspiration and application with or without the underlying knowledge of chakra theory and labyrinths. That is why an easily accessible version is presented in this chapter. I have included the underlying theory and a more thorough description of the maps in the Appendix. That is meant both as reference and as an illustration of how XIPs – in this case, me – will often connect various fields of knowledge to come up with new applications when they want to apply their Xi. Let me illustrate the importance of both subjects with the following:

> *Chakra theory has been of deep interest to me for more than two decades. Although originally typically Eastern knowledge, Western writers have made the link with Western psychology (Judith, 1996). This theory has helped me to develop my intuitive qualities, to increase my self-confidence, and to improve my body-mind balance.*
> *Labyrinths entered my life about the same time as the subject of giftedness, around 1999. I was invited to walk one and experienced there and then that my restless mind quieted down in the labyrinth. I felt more solidly connected to my body, standing with both feet on the ground, as well as inspired with insight as to why labyrinths were important to me.*

Chakras are energy nodes situated at specific locations in our body.
The seven major chakras are located from the base of our spine (first chakra) to the top of our head (seventh chakra). Since the energy frequency increases from the lowest chakra up to the highest chakra, often the colours of the rainbow are used to characterize them: From red for the first chakra (bottom of spine), via orange, yellow, green, turquoise and indigo, to violet for the seventh chakra (top of head).
Each chakra correlates with specific states of consciousness, from physical security and health to spiritual awareness. More information on chakras can be found in the Appendix.

A *labyrinth* is a meandering path, corresponding to a very old rhythmic structure or pattern. One can draw a labyrinth on paper, and follow the path with a finger. One can also create it life-size somewhere on the ground, and walk it. This gives a stronger effect, as one's entire body makes circular movements and is moved by them. Walking a labyrinth is a practical and validated tool to improve one's connection between mind and body, to come to decisions on personal issues and regain energy to implement them – in short – to facilitate finding one's true expression. Walking a labyrinth is also a means to come to rest and enjoyment. More information on labyrinths can be found in the Appendix, and on my website www.willemlabyrint.nl.

The pattern used is named the "Classical seven-circuit labyrinth pattern." The image shows the meandering path in various shades of grey, between the thinly lined borders.

The path to the centre takes you along seven *circuits* in a certain sequence. If the circuits are numbered from the outside inwards, the sequence of the path is 3-2-1-4-7-6-5-centre. The path outwards has the inverse sequence.

In my maps, I use the colours of the rainbow from the outside inwards to designate the different circuits. These colours match the colours of the seven chakras, and the significance of each circuit is related to the corresponding chakra. There is a full colour illustration of the rainbow labyrinth on the back cover.

The maps of figure 15 and 16 illustrate how the process of expression can be compared to walking a labyrinth:

- each circuit is related to and influences a specific aspect of that process;
- in each circuit the process can continue its flow or become stagnated;
- both walking to the centre and returning by the same path correspond to the various aspects of the actual process of expression;
- the labyrinth can be walked in the mind but also physically in a life-size labyrinth.

The maps make one aware of what kinds of stagnation exist and what the flow counterparts are about. They indicate the theoretical direction out of that specific stagnation.

Using the map for actually walking a labyrinth offers the practical approach to reflect – while physically moving – on personal flow and stagnation in one's personal expression. It is our experience that concentrating on the walking of a specific circuit, which is connected to someone's personal point of stagnation, may help in overcoming that stagnation and reconnecting to a flowing expression.

Please refer to the Appendix for more explanation on the maps and on the labyrinths of stagnation and of flowing expression.

Figure 15: The labyrinth of stagnation

Yellow	I must/should make a start with something…
Orange	It is my fault if anything goes wrong…
Red	It will never be good enough…
Green	Nobody wants to be with me, neither do I…
Violet	It is all utterly meaningless…
Indigo	I don't understand it at all, I'm confused…
Turquoise	I'd better keep quiet…
Pink	Another failure…

The return path may be heavy with regret and grief.
Or it can be used as an opportunity for coming to terms with all this.

Figure 16: The labyrinth of flowing expression

Yellow	Yes, I want to take the first step now.
Orange	I have a good gut feeling about it.
Red	I am solidly grounded and full of energy.
Green	I have a good rapport with my environment.
Violet	I am receptive for inspiration and unhindered by limiting convictions.
Indigo	My mind is clear, I have my vision.
Turquoise	I do as I do.
Pink	I have done.

The return path is meant for reflection, satisfaction and recharging of the batteries.

Chapter 8 *Living happily ever after as an XIP*

Is it safe to accept being an XIP?

After many pages of caveats and complexities regarding the application of one's Xi, one might wonder whether it is a good idea, after all, to make explicit being an XIP both to oneself and to one's environment.
Making it explicit might make the subject bigger than it needs to be.
This could complicate the application of Xi and diminish personal effectiveness. That was not the intention, was it?

Carol Dweck (2006) reports that a most consistent outcome of seven experiments with hundreds of children is:

> *Praising children's intelligence harms their motivation and their performance. (p. 170) Of course children need praise, like everyone else, but praise them for their efforts and learning, not for their intelligence, effortless speed or perfection.*

That leads to the question whether a notion about "*extra* intelligence" is principally ill-conceived.

Practical evidence shows that there are differences in intelligence between people and that - independent of mindset - different patterns of personal qualities exist, depending on their intelligence in the widest sense.
Our intention with the introduction of the concept of Xi and XIPs was:
An easy accessible means to help a certain minority discover their specific "personal manual," given the fact that they seemed to need various additional sections in their manual that the majority do not need at all.
Therefore we decided to coin a concept that one needs to take into ownership oneself – not as the result of a judgment by a professional expert, but by one's own choice and assessment.

We hoped and expected that the essential recognition of three or more out of the five characteristics of Xi would trigger individual curiosity to learn more about oneself. Similarly, recognizing somebody else in the description

would enable the observer to get a different understanding of that person's needs and behaviour. Such an observer might even encourage the other to find out more about Xi and himself/herself.
Promoting curiosity and stimulating personal development sounds like the growth mindset.

The possibility of being uncommonly intelligent is not obvious or easily acceptable for every XIP: However, only one of the five characteristics of Xi is about being smart, or rather *behaving* smart (it has to be recognizable).
We have met many clients who only grudgingly allowed for the possibility that they might, after all, be relatively smart but had come to us in the first place because of their stunning recognition of the other characteristics of Xi in themselves. Often their school career had been a disaster and they had vivid memories of being told they were dumb and/or lazy.
Only when they found out *how* they were uncommonly smart, and acknowledged the extended definition of multiple intelligences, did the recognition of the characteristic of being extra intelligent became acceptable to them. Some, however, kept being very sceptical about their own intelligence.
For them it was more manageable to refer to their Xi as extra *intensity*.
In all cases, however, their need for autonomy, their exceptionable inquisitiveness and zeal in finding ways to grow and learn, "betrayed" them convincingly as being an XIP. That is also what stimulated them to personally investigate the body of knowledge about XIPs and find out what profit they could derive from it for themselves.

We have no doubts about our own intention to foster growth and increase the effectiveness of XIPs. After all, we have only been able to formulate our knowledge about Xi after having discovered it personally step by step. Sometimes it has also cost us considerable frustration before effort yielded new insight. And it must be mentioned that we learned many things through our clients. Working with the concept of Xi has in no way kept us from practicing a growth mindset; long before we knew of the mindset theory.

There will always be people that will react aversely to expressing the statement *"I am an XIP"* because they feel strangled or pinned down by this label, even if the characteristics of Xi fit them evidently and very strongly so.

On the other hand, some people feel that the abbreviation *XIP* makes the situation sound friendlier, like belonging to a nice and somehow funny group of people. They do not experience the label as having to be special, but just as a fair description of being different in some respect, while still wanting to live in a world with XIPs and non-XIPs. We consider it just another example of the diversity of XIPs.

As long as one allows everybody space and time to recognize and acknowledge being an XIP, and to take their own responsibility for the consequences, I feel the concept is not pushing XIPs into a fixed mindset; in fact, the contrary is true. Knowledge about the power of mindsets, however, should encourage every XIP to listen very carefully to the kind of praise one is offered by many – mostly well-meaning – people. Since "being smart" is traditionally a strong wish of many people, they may inadvertently shower you with their praise about your being brilliant. They may think that "extra intelligent" confirms that you are very, *very* intelligent.

Even if this might actually be true, be aware of the possible stifling effects the remark may have on you, jeopardizing the application of your Xi:

> *It may effectively deprive you of your dear and sometimes hard-won mindset of jumping on opportunities, working late, making mistakes and learning from them, and behaving sometimes completely unpredictably.*

But most of all, it should be realized that the acknowledgement of being an XIP is only the first step: important, but not the whole story. A label like XIP is just the envelope around the real message – *how* you are an XIP and how you are *applying* your Xi.
To my experience it is almost always more effective to be specific about the relevant aspects of your Xidentity, than on the XIP issue as such. Xidentity characteristics can be explained to others in normal language and are verifiable by the other, even if they are quite extraordinary as such.

Yes, it is safe to accept being an XIP. No, it is not a suit of armour that protects you, nor one that will restrain your movements while protecting you.

The Effective XIP, a Work in Progress

Effectiveness is not static, but a permanent balancing of needs for personal development and needs for practical results of one's efforts, a balancing of input and output.

The personal development of an XIP is a dynamic process: both quantitatively through acquired experience and qualitatively through changes in Xidentity. Consider for example the effects of Xinasty, extra receptiveness (Xr) and development of autonomy, or the balance between task-orientation and empathy (Xt and Xe).
Personal efforts and results may change dynamically too. Just think of:

- development of new interdisciplinary fields;
- creation of new bodies of knowledge;
- shifts of personal interest.

Similarly the workplace environment may change considerably through a change of management, reorganizations, mergers, or national changes.

I have often compared XIPs to a precision instrument – made for special, often complicated tasks, but delicate by nature.
XIPs need careful tuning and proper maintenance to keep themselves in perfect condition. It is definitely worthwhile to do so, from the point of view of both the XIP and of their environment.
The three Practices are meant as practical tools to facilitate this process of balanced progression in becoming more effective.

Yes, XIPs can make a difference!

Living happily ever after as an XIP

Georgina is sitting autonomously and at ease in her own Ximension. She has her unique and charming way of directing her environment to make things happen naturally.
It was through her that Annelien and I got interested in giftedness and were prompted to think of new ways to connect this subject to the personal development of adults.
I am very happy and grateful to witness her work in progress.

Paul made this picture of me as part of his series of XIPs and added the following commentary: "I wanted to make a portrait of Willem while he is expressing his skills: Explaining a theory that he has formulated after careful investigations. Seated behind his desk he explained his idea to me while I was making photographs. This is to me part of his excellence."

Appendix 1: A case of applying Xi

This Appendix is an illustration of the third Practice: an XIP, in this case, myself *applying Xi*.
It is also the extensive reference to the content of the last section of chapter seven, *A map of stagnation and flowing expression*.

> In 2008 I felt the urge to work out a new approach to the process of personal expression by combining different bodies of knowledge. I had joined our new course for XIPs, called Training Mastery. It had been conceived and started by Annelien in cooperation with artists Paul Rüpp and Mariska Mallee. The aim of the Training is to increase consciously the mastery of personal expression, using various creative means like painting and photographing.
> In our first book I had used the labyrinth as a metaphor of the various stages in the process of achieving excellence. I had already collected a lot of information on the relation between the labyrinth circuits and the seven chakras. Could I come up with a relevant description of the relation between expression, labyrinths and chakras to facilitate the conscious embodiment of the process of expression?
>
> There was, however, a complicating circumstance. The Training Mastery was supposed to come to its peak by the end of September with every participant presenting a "material expression" in the shop-window of KunstRaam (ArtWindow), the studio of Paul and Mariska. I had joined the Training out of curiosity and because Annelien had started it. But what could I possibly present in a shop-window? Everyone made efforts to encourage me and express their confidence, which made me feel only worse. All summer I was quite depressed about it.
> Early September, the evening before the last day of the training, I reflected on and wrote down why I hated these kinds of situations and why I had hated them all my life. It actually reminded me of earlier embarrassing moments of feeling powerless and unable to meet other people's expectations.
>
> In these dark hours, I suddenly realized how my personal stagnation matched with the theme of specific circuits of the labyrinth and their chakra counterparts. I scribbled it down, and went to bed.

> Next morning I polished the concept using consistent terminology for all circuits and chakras and the labyrinth of stagnation was discovered!
> The labyrinth of flowing expression proved to be a variation of the version in my first book. Finding a visual way of presenting these results in the shop-window was relatively easy, and I enjoyed presenting my new concepts during a special workshop. It was well received.
> Afterwards, I expanded the various elements of the concept, and made illustrations that suited my taste and purpose. The results can be found in the next sections of this Appendix.

The first two sections offer a concise explanation of the relevant aspects of chakra theory and of the characteristics of a seven-circuit labyrinth.
Then I expand on the dynamics of a flowing expression, while the last section offers a view of the way expression can stagnate.

THE BODY AND THE MIND, A BRIEF INTRO ON CHAKRAS

All my life, I have been interested in finding out and understanding how my body and my mind are mirrored in each other and what spirit means for both. Although I am well aware that for many people and scientists this is not in line with their views, to me there are three reasons why this subject can be very meaningful to XIPs and influence their effectiveness:

1. I physically experience the tight relation between my state of mind and the state of my body, and through taking this relationship seriously I keep my balance.
2. In the same vein, connecting with heaven and earth through specific exercises keeps my body and mind well aligned between them, and provides an important source of sparkling energy and inspiration.
3. When people meet, there is not only an exchange of ideas and/or physical contact, but also an exchange of personal energies. Due to their intensity, XIPs (and especially extra empathic [Xe] ones like myself) can experience strong effects and after-effects of these exchanges and should be aware of how to note and handle these.

Chakra theory offers a kind of map to depict and explore these relationships. Chakras are located at specific places in the body; their energy states reflect our emotional and mental processes and their flows of energy connect us with heaven and earth.

It is introduced here both as a reference to instruments for XIPs to "maintain their precision instrument," and as a map for describing the dynamics of expression and stagnation in the next sections.

A serious limitation of the description is that these words and images can only convey the *map*, while the actual experience of the *territory* will make explicit what this approach can mean to the reader and his/her personal expression. However, the map serves its purpose of communicating the issue.

What are chakras?

There are many books about chakras, and they do not always agree with each other. Some are more esoteric than others. I prefer the ones that link Eastern knowledge about the human body with Western psychology (Judith, 1996/2004).

For the purpose of this book the following aspects seem most relevant:

- A chakra is a kind of spinning wheel or vortex of energy;
- There are seven major chakras at specific locations in our body, from the base of our spine to the top of our head (see figure 17);
- These seven chakras correlate with specific states of consciousness;
- The chakra at the base of the spine is called first chakra; the one on top of our head is the seventh chakra;
- The energy frequency of the first chakra is lowest and increases upwards until the seventh chakra. This can be symbolized by the seven colours of the rainbow, from red, via orange, yellow, green, turquoise and indigo to violet;
- Our chakras change in the course of our lives, the way our physical body changes. Chakras contain information on various life experiences, including traumatic ones.

Each chakra shows through its condition one's actual functioning in two ways:

- A chakra can be more or less open and actively receiving and emanating energy, which shows itself in the correlated mind and body domain;

- The condition of the chakra influences the amount of flow through two vertical currents of energy: The liberating current that ascends through the chakras and the manifesting current that descends through them. In that way the condition of one chakra can influence the condition of its neighbours.

Characteristics of each of the seven chakras

Each chakra can be characterized by various aspects. In this brief intro we can only give an impression.
The chakras are described from the first to the seventh, from the base of the spine to the top of the head. See also figure 17: The location of the seven chakras on the body.

1st chakra
The first chakra is located at the base of our spine, and is the most earthly and fleshly of the seven. Its corresponding element is earth, its colour red.
Its theme is survival, security, stability, physical health and prosperity.

2nd chakra
The second chakra is located in the abdomen, below the navel. Its element is water, which is less dense than earth, its colour orange.
Its theme includes emotions, sexuality, vitality, mobility and passion.

3rd chakra
The third chakra is located above the navel, at the solar plexus. Its element is fire, a driving force, and its colour yellow.
Its theme is willpower and force, energy, autonomy and individuality.

4th chakra
The fourth chakra is located at the heart. It is the middle chakra and it connects the relatively concrete lower three chakras with the relatively abstract upper three. This is where body and mind, where substance and spirit meet. The metaphor that our essence, our soul lives in our heart expresses that idea.
Its element is air, its colour green.
Its theme is love and relationships, social identity, compassion and devotion.

Appendix 1: A Case of Applying Xi

Figure 17: The location of the seven chakras on the body

5th chakra
The fifth chakra is located at the throat, the relatively narrow bridge between torso and head. Its element is sound, its colour turquoise.
Its theme is communication, creativity, listening, resonance and expression.

6th chakra
The sixth chakra is located at the middle of the brow, often called the third eye. The element is light; its colour is indigo, a dark blue.
Its theme is imagination, intuition and vision, as well as balance between left and right aspects of our body.

7th chakra
The seventh chakra is located at the top of our head, and it is the most spiritual and abstract of the seven. Its element is thought, its colour violet.
Its theme is awareness, spirituality, transcendence, universality, but also dogma and other belief systems.

The vertical currents of energy

We live on the boundary between heaven and earth, and are influenced by both. In many cultural traditions, heaven and earth are linked to masculine and feminine, as they are linked to spirit and substance.

The upward *current of liberation* is a primitive force of raw energy that puts substance in motion. Its power makes plants break through tarmac or mortar, and gives the season of spring its impetuous character. It is the energy component for the transformation of substance through personal growth and expansion into conscious acting and being in the widest sense.
Its force can be felt in everyone's body, but the intensity of the current at the different chakra locations varies from person to person and from time to time.

The downward *current of manifestation* is an ordering force, which gives spirit its embodiment through personal significance, expression and ultimately grounding. Inspirational thoughts and ideas are systemized, linked to context, and gradually become more real and tangible leading towards their materialization in the physical world.

It is the structuring component for the transformation of inspiration into its material realisation in time and space.
Everyone can experience this inspiration, but also this current's intensity at the different chakra locations varies also from person to person and from time to time.

The two currents influence the chakras they pass, and are influenced by their state. One needs them both. If there is no raw energy rising upwards, there is nothing to order or structure for the current of manifestation: ideas remain ideas. If there is no structured inspiration, the upward current of liberation is just "much ado about nothing": commotion, but no progress.

Taking mind and body to a labyrinth

A labyrinth is a meandering path, corresponding to a very old rhythmic structure or pattern. Walking a labyrinth helps to focus on personal themes and to come to new insights, but also to come to rest and enjoyment.
It is a practical tool to improve one's connection between mind and body, to come to decisions on personal issues and regain energy to implement them – in short – to facilitate finding one's true expression.
Before explaining their structure and meaning, I will give a short interlude to explain the importance to our process of finding our own expression.

> As I mentioned earlier, labyrinths entered my life at about the same time as the subject of giftedness, around 1999. I was invited to walk one and experienced there and then that my restless mind quieted down in the labyrinth. I felt both more solidly connected to my body, standing with both feet on the ground, and inspired with insight about why labyrinths were important to me.
> As a mathematician, the beauty of the pattern and its effects intrigued me. As an engineer, I started to build labyrinths and to try out variations of design. Around 2005, I discovered the masculine aspects of the labyrinth, and their influence on the creative process of labyrinth building. In 2007 I found the connection between the various paths of a labyrinth and the process of career coaching and wrote about it in my first book. In 2008 both Annelien and I used it in our Training Mastery. While working on it, I discovered its application to the process of stagnation.

The pattern of a labyrinth

The labyrinth pattern of figure 18 is the Classical seven-circuit labyrinth. The first documentation of this pattern is on a Greek clay tablet of more than 3000 years ago.

Some people prefer to draw the separating borders of the path, also known as the *walls* of the labyrinth, the upper picture of the three. If one enters the labyrinth at the bottom of the graph between the black lines, called the *mouth* of the labyrinth, the *path* meanders left and right as depicted in the lower picture through the coloured line.

The middle picture unites the patterns of walls and path.

The path to the centre takes you along seven *circuits* in a certain sequence. If the circuits are numbered from the outside inwards, the sequence of the path is 3-2-1-4-7-6-5-centre.

The colours used are the colours of the rainbow, which were already introduced in the previous section to characterize the seven chakras. The colour of the centre is pink, the colour of unconditional love.

Each circuit has a certain symbolic significance, and the sequence of the circuits as induced through the pattern, leads to a process of reflection, relaxation, unburdening, and inspiration.

Put in a table, the sequence is as follows:

Table 4: Labyrinth circuit, theme and colour

Circuit	Theme	Colour
3	what do I want	yellow
2	how does it feel	orange
1	confrontation with reality	red
4	who do I want to be with	green
7	what is my purpose	violet
6	what is my idea / plan	indigo
5	I do as I do	turquoise
centre	I have done	pink

Appendix 1: A Case of Applying Xi   155

Figure 18: Classical labyrinth: pattern, path and its combination

One can walk the labyrinth without worries of getting lost: Keeping on the path brings one to the centre. The *walls* are usually just a low separation, not a high hedge that obstructs an overview of the situation. The alternation of turning left and right brings balance and stimulates creativity. The labyrinth is a safe space, often even a sacred space.

The way out means following the same path in reverse. Most people reflect on their experiences of the inward journey and their stay in the centre. Often they emerge from the mouth feeling energized and ready for action. This is one of the reasons why it is important to make that outward journey too, instead of just sneaking out.

The Dynamics of expression

Expression of excellence is a process that takes time to carry through. The "excellent result" is an important part of this process. But with the concept of effectiveness in mind – desired results, obtained in a sustainable way – it is only logical that there is more to working towards expression than focusing on the result of it.

By 2007 I had discovered that the process of excellent expression could be compared to the process of walking a labyrinth. In 2008 I found out how knowledge of chakras and the two vertical currents of energy, combined with the labyrinth, offered more detailed insight into the dynamics of expression and the pitfalls that lead to stagnation.
This description of the process is a kind of excerpt from the actual processes that take often a much longer time span to carry out: One can brood for some time on an idea, or chew on a problem, until inevitably, the "time has come." Of course during all that time of brooding and chewing, chakras have been active, currents flowing, and so on. The feeling that time has come is linked here to the decision of entering the labyrinth. I focus on what will happen then.

At first glance, expression is about realisation of an idea, therefore something connected with the downward current of manifestation. But expression is more than acting on some idea to throw a stone in a pond. The upward current of raw energy that allows growth and expansion is an essential source of energy to make the idea come to life.

Moving upwards and downwards is symbolized in a labyrinth by moving to a circuit that is closer to, or respectively more distant from, the centre. Walking a specific circuit is linked to the corresponding chakra and the experiencing of its theme, either in a stimulating or in a frustrating way.

The patterns of possible stagnation

The process of expression does not always evolve unhampered. Although one – at the actual moment of stagnation – certainly feels down and out, stagnation at its best offers possibilities for real personal growth and for overcoming limiting patterns in one's biography. When this process of overcoming lasts a considerable time and expression stagnates in the same measure, unfortunately, it is hard to put on a happy face.

However, this is also when and where the added value of the labyrinth as a model or metaphor of the process of expression becomes more visible:
By adding language to the various stages of the process, it is possible to be more aware of, and more specific about the actual reasons for stagnation and their implications. This can contribute to finding a clue or seeking help to do something about the situation.
Additionally, by using the labyrinth physically, whether by walking it, drawing it, or by tracing the path with a finger, it is possible to connect mind and body in the perception of the stagnation. In the same vein, one can experiment with ways specific for mind or body to overcome stagnation and use the labyrinth to resynchronize the two.
For the record: this appendix will not cover all possible forms of stagnation, but still a nasty lot.

Enter the Shadow

Stagnation often has to do with one's Shadow aspects, the Jungian description for the collection of personal qualities that one does not like to be reminded about. American poet and author Robert Bly (1998) tells us in his book the powerful story of *"The Long Bag We Drag Behind Us."*

> *Behind us we have an invisible bag, and the part of us our parents don't like, we, to keep our parents' love, put in the bag.... Then we do a lot of bag stuffing in high school.... We spend our life until we're twenty deciding*

what parts of ourselves to put into the bag, and we spend the rest of our lives trying to get them out again...

Often it is not so easy to get those parts out again, especially when they have been inside for a long time. The way a guard dog, living tethered to his kennel, gradually becomes more mean and angry, those long-hidden parts of ourselves in our bag bark and bite when we try to get them out. It takes courage and patience to persevere in bringing them into the light and befriending them again.

In the metaphor of "the long bag we drag behind us," we can indeed get stuck in one of the circuits of the labyrinth, and can only proceed when we have made the bag less bulky. Of course this takes time and effort but it is very worthwhile to go for it, because the bag becomes lighter to drag, leaving us with more energy and agility to continue our path.
And, wonderfully apt, walking a labyrinth has always been connected to the process of releasing old burdens, and being revived with fresh inspiration.

Another easily imaginable aspect of stagnation in a certain circuit is its effect on the flow of the currents of manifestation and liberation. When stagnation occurs, the flow is hampered and a kind of reservoir builds up, especially upsetting the previous circuit and the balance of its connected chakra. Thus, where in the labyrinth of expression the flow of both currents is strengthened after each passing of a chakra, the hampered flow of a current weakens the upstream chakra as well.
This effect will be clarified for every circuit of the labyrinth's path.

A special warning for XIPs on the reading of this section is, however, appropriate: Due to their tendency of perfectionism, and their critical minds, it is almost tempting to recognize in oneself every cause for stagnation in the following explanation for the various circuits and the connecting chakras.

> When I first read the book of Anodea Judith (1996) on the chakras and their possible development, I found myself "guilty on all elements of the accusation." My urge for personal development almost worked like an executioner chopping my head off (or, more correctly, chopping my body off, while my head argued on). Writing about stagnation was quite contagious too.

The biggest challenge was to convince myself that this approach was valid and valuable. But frankly, what do you think of it? Oops, sorry...

Please treat yourself and your "bag" gently and lovingly. Just continue dragging it carefully behind you, and perhaps the time has come to look at just one of its inhabitants more closely, trying to re-establish contact.

THE PATH OF FLOWING EXPRESSION AND OF POSSIBLE STAGNATION

The purpose of this section is to offer a map that may lead you through difficult terrain. But there can be no doubt that braving the territory of the desert or of the caves is the actual experience that will make the difference. If you encounter possible stagnation, only the actual experience will offer the opportunity to reconnect to an inhabitant of your bag of shadows and make it lighter.

The structure of this section follows the path through the circuits of the labyrinth. For every circuit I give a short description of its character and meaning. Then both the connected experiences while in a state of flowing expression or of possible stagnation are explained.

I choose to address the reader directly to enhance the experience of actually walking through the labyrinth. One may start reading this section by omitting the stagnation elements, just to get the idea of flowing expression. Afterwards, as felt needed, the applicable stagnation elements may offer an explanation for personal experiences from the past or present.

The third circuit

Upon entering the labyrinth, the path takes you straight to the third circuit. This is connected to the third chakra, coloured yellow, the chakra of force and willpower, autonomy and individuality.

FLOWING EXPRESSION

Expression starts with willing: Feeling the strength of your autonomy, you confirm in this circuit to yourself that you will go for something, and that this something is important to you.

SIGNS OF POSSIBLE STAGNATION

You feel compelled to start on a task that you don't consider your own plan, idea or wish but someone else's decision. It drains your energy. It impedes your feeling of autonomy. Your own downward current of manifestation does not inspire you; it looks more like a sideways insertion or force.
This is particularly a weak point of Extra Empathic People. They tend to feel obliged to fulfil other's wishes. Prolonged stagnation may result in excessive extra empathic behaviour and co-dependency.

The second circuit

At the end of the third circuit, the path turns outwards and takes you to the second circuit. This is connected to the second chakra, coloured orange, the chakra of emotions and vitality, of mobility and passion.
Be aware that your attention is moving downwards in your body, flowing with the current of manifestation.

FLOWING EXPRESSION

You investigate your feelings about this expression of excellence.
You feel your body react and move accordingly. This strengthens your confidence: It is time for the change!

SIGNS OF POSSIBLE STAGNATION

Instead of feeling confident, you fear to get the blame when something goes wrong. It is far too risky to try something different or new. Your spirits sink and you avoid contact with others and their guilt-invoking reproaches like: "You are always so…"
The hampered current of manifestation may upset your earlier willpower: "You never wanted to do it in the first place." All adding up to your frozen state of doing and feeling.

The first circuit

At the end of the second circuit, the path again turns outwards and takes you to the first, the most outer circuit. This is connected to the first chakra, coloured red, the chakra of safety, security and stability, and also of physical health and prosperity.

The current of manifestation reaches its lowest, most concrete point in your body.

FLOWING EXPRESSION

Are you feeling grounded and secure, very fit to provide a stable base for your idea to be put into the world, to be materialized? You have already decided to do it, and it felt good to take the next step. In this circuit, if the logistics are available and everything is checked and OK, you are definitely ready for "take off."

SIGNS OF POSSIBLE STAGNATION

One form of stagnation is an existential unsafe feeling: Unsure of your basic right of existence on the face of the earth, you do not dare to let the current of manifestation touch ground. "It will be no good anyway." The stopped downward current builds a reservoir and unbalances your previous confidence: "And it is all my fault."

Another form of stagnation arises from fear of insufficient quality of your expression: "It will be not good enough, I need more ... before I can continue." This stagnation affects the upward current of liberation, preventing it from emerging, in fact preventing "liberation." Everything is taken too seriously.

Introverted, very brainy XIPs may be vulnerable: Their mind is limitless, their bodily actions relatively slow and imperfect. One needs to trust the data of all one's senses to engage "the real world" and build whatever is possible.

The fourth circuit

At the end of the first circuit, the path turns inwards and takes you in one big turn halfway the centre, to the fourth circuit. This is connected to the fourth chakra, coloured green, the chakra of connection, love and devotion, which connects earth and heaven, body and mind, outside and inside.

FLOWING EXPRESSION

Expression feels like a firm and fluid stretching on the upward current of liberation, like standing up to take your place between heaven and earth. It is also the place to consider balance between inside and outside. The first three circuits were about yourself: your decision, feeling and stability.

On your way up, this is the moment to be aware of being a person among other people, and the consequences of interdependence.
It can be the moment to decide with whom you will travel further, or to accept sub-persons within yourself as valuable aspects of your essence.

SIGNS OF POSSIBLE STAGNATION

Stagnation has to do with feeling unconnected and alone, grieving.
The help you had expected has not arrived or was not what you expected. You wish you could share your worries with someone, but are afraid to ask and be rejected. You may also feel disconnected to your own body, where what you think and what you do differs widely and unexpectedly.
The stagnation of the upward current of liberation may unbalance the upstream chakras three, two and one, weakening your focus, depriving you of your vitality and joy of life, and urging you to make (endlessly) more preparations before continuing your process of expression.

The seventh circuit

At the end of the fourth circuit, the path makes the second big turn inwards and takes you to the – very short – seventh circuit, closest to the centre. This circuit is connected to the seventh chakra, located at the crown of your head, coloured violet, the chakra of awareness and spirituality but also of dogma and belief systems.

FLOWING EXPRESSION

The upward current of liberation has reached its highest point in your body. All raw energy has joined in to make your original idea or plan grow and expand within the limits of your own body and mind system. Now is the time to be ready to receive something new, some inspiration, a new level or perspective of your work at hand. Keep your hands ready to catch what will fall into them. Don't look until you know you have secured the catch.

SIGNS OF POSSIBLE STAGNATION

Stagnation brings about the idea of: "What's the use of my expression, it is meaningless to continue" and lots of rational or irrational arguments to support that limiting conviction. No inspiration is perceived nor received. Everything remains as it was.
The stagnation of the upward current of liberation may unbalance the

upstream chakras six and five, leading to chaotic thinking and muting of expression and communication.
When the downward current of manifestation stagnates too, due to all kinds of convictions about the current situation that prevent from going with the flow, the process of expression is crippled.

The sixth circuit

At the end of the short seventh circuit, you turn outwards to the neighbouring sixth circuit. This circuit is connected to the sixth chakra, coloured indigo, the chakra of imagination, intuition and vision. Again you are following the current of manifestation, but now on
a more abstract level: how to interpret the received inspiration. However, all the work done before reaching this seventh circuit is still present in your mind and body.

FLOWING EXPRESSION

If the chakra is sufficiently clear and focused, suddenly all pieces of the puzzle fall to their right places. Yes!
The "engine" of the current of liberation is warm and running, and there is clarity about the intention of the current of manifestation. Now is the time for the actual expression!

SIGNS OF POSSIBLE STAGNATION

Your mind is not clear or focused, and all the information keeps spinning around in your head unfiltered and delusional. "I do not understand what to do, which way to go, what to choose. Everything is messed up."
The hampered current of manifestation upsets the seventh chakra: "But why bother? It is all meaningless." A drain of energy and no output.

The fifth circuit

At the end of the sixth circuit, you turn outwards to the neighbouring fifth circuit. This circuit is connected to the fifth chakra, coloured turquoise, the chakra of communication and creativity, of resonance and expression. The chakra is located in the throat area and also connects to the mobility of shoulders, arms and hands.

FLOWING EXPRESSION

Are you ready to express, to tell the world, to gesture, to articulate your creation? If all is well, you can say: "I do as I do," regardless of the results of your excellent expression. Assessment and analysis will come later.
Now is the time to enjoy and relax before going back through the labyrinth: Move on towards the centre; we are only halfway!

SIGNS OF POSSIBLE STAGNATION

Stagnation mutes your voice and suppresses your expression. Invitations and supportive remarks are not considered or heard. Instead of "I do as I do" it is: "If I just keep quiet or go away, perhaps no one will notice me or my absence." The hampered current of manifestation upsets the sixth chakra, obscuring your vision and muddling your thinking, making a proper assessment of the situation almost impossible. The opportunity is lost.

The centre

At the end of the fifth circuit, the path makes a big turn inwards to reach the centre of the labyrinth. Traditionally the place to rest and be nourished. There are only seven big chakras, but some suggest an eighth chakra, near the heart chakra.

FLOWING EXPRESSION

In a way you step out of the active process of expression and take a rest to celebrate. When you are ready, it is time for the journey back. This is an important part of the process, as it gives you opportunities to interpret what has happened up to now, and to learn from it.
However, we will sketch this part of the journey more briefly.

SIGNS OF POSSIBLE STAGNATION

When stagnation has occurred, there may be bitterness and resentment, even anger for "having failed again."
Often no time is taken for a proper rest, because there is no time to lose:
You have to retry immediately and correct your failures. But that involves a big risk of restarting just because you *have to*, instead of restarting because you have *decided* to do so.

The way back

The way back is literally the return road. All circuits are travelled in the reverse order: Fifth, sixth and seventh circuit, than the "jump" via the fourth circuit to the first circuit, then second and third circuit, and the path ends outside the labyrinth.

On this return road, the current of *liberation* is most prominent. Given the recent experience of expression, the chakras that are passed (fifth, sixth, seventh, and first, second, third) remember through reflection what has happened and record this information in the chakra. Through the process this vital upward current becomes in a way positively conditioned for a next time.

FLOWING EXPRESSION

Leaving the *centre*, you re-enter the *fifth circuit* and realise the meaning of creativity, and how it works for you. You might want to express it and tell others about it.

In the *sixth circuit* you can look in retrospection to the information filtering process that has made you form your opinions, and consider making changes for the future. Or a new idea is formed, to work on at a later time.

The *seventh circuit* takes just a moment to walk. There is, however, time to consider the value of inspiration and the way it gives meaning to your life force. Additionally you may consider whether old belief systems have become obsolete and welcome new ones.

In a fast movement, following the current of manifestation, you move through the *fourth circuit* to the most outward, first circuit. It manifests like a lightning bolt your awareness of the relevance of our position between heaven and earth. In this movement you walk calmly the fourth circuit and consider the value of connecting to others and yourself and how your expression has influenced that connection.

While walking the *first circuit*, you ponder the impact of your expression on the world, and re-establish its right of existence. What is your reward?

While moving upwards on the current of liberation, in the *second circuit* you wildly enjoy the materialisation of your expression. It feels really good and all your senses are attuned.

In the *third circuit*, your joy joins your feeling of performance and success, and in a winning mood you burst out of the labyrinth.

Reflecting on and Learning of Possible Stagnation

Just stepping out of the labyrinth instead of walking the way back may prolong the stagnation. "I have failed, so it's no use walking back."
Alternatively, if you are willing to take the way back, there will be many opportunities to reflect on and learn about what has happened as was illustrated in the previous text.

Walking the labyrinth is taking the process of expression to the next level. But, unfortunately, stretching one's limits does not always work out immediately the way one would like. The possibility to physically walk the path of expression – while moving one's body – offers extra protection against possible risks of stagnation.
Please consider that, after all, stagnation is not unnatural or evil. It is often just an opportunity to grow. However – to my own experience – the nicest part of stagnation is when it has been overcome and the bag full of shadows has become less bulky again. That is certainly my wish to you.
Then we can continue our path lightened and with fresh inspiration.
Just another day to enjoy the gift of being uncommon.

Appendix 2: Personal reflections on Xi

I mention five characteristics of eXtra intelligence, Xi, in chapter one.

How do you relate to these characteristics?

Please circle your preference.

	measure of recognition			
	very	good	fair	hardly
Intellectually able	x	x	x	x
Incurably inquisitive	x	x	x	x
Needs autonomy	x	x	x	x
Excessive zeal in pursuit of interests	x	x	x	x
Contrast between emotional and intellectual self-confidence	x	x	x	x

Is your interest in the subject of Xi related to:

Your current employment	yes	somewhat	no
Finding new employment	yes	somewhat	no
Your profession (HRM, management)	yes	somewhat	no
Your personal development	yes	somewhat	no
Family or friends	yes	somewhat	no

Name: ....
Organization: ....
Position: ....
Age: .... m / f

Thank you.

References

Advanced Development: A Journal on Adult Giftedness. (1989-). Various articles. Denver, CO, USA: Institute for the Study of Advanced Development.

Baron-Cohen, S. (2003). *The Essential Difference.* London, England: Penguin Books.

Berens, L.V. (2006). *An Introduction to the 4 Temperaments 3.0* (Understanding yourself and others series). Huntington Beach, CA, USA: Telos Publications.

Bly, R. (1988). *A Little Book on the Human Shadow.* New York, NY, USA: HarperCollins.

Cameron, K.S. and Quinn, R.E. (2006). *Diagnosing and Changing Organizational Culture.* San Francisco, CA, USA: Jossey-Bass.

Covey, S.R. (2004). *The 8th Habit: From Effectiveness to Greatness.* London, England: Simon & Schuster.

Dweck, C.S. (2006). *Mindset: the new psychology of success.* New York, NY, USA: Random House.

Ensing-Wijn, M.E. (2006). *Alles stroomt...Een nadere beschouwing van het fenomeen Beelddenken (Everything flows...Looking closer at the fenomenon of imaginal thinking).* Wassenaar, the Netherlands: M.J. Krabbe Stichting.

Gardner, H. (1999). *Intelligence Reframed: Multiple Intelligences for the 21st Century.* New York, NY, USA: Basic Books.

Geffen, G. van. (2007). *Verschil moet er zijn: de kritische succesfactoren voor diversiteitsmanagement (Making the Difference: critical successfactors in diversity management).* Amsterdam, the Netherlands: Business Contact. (English version of the book will be published end of 2010.)

Hyde, L. (2007). *The Gift: Creativity and the Artist in the Modern World.* New York, NY, USA: Vintage Books.

Iacoboni, M. (2008). *Mirroring People - The New Science of How We Connect With Others.* New York, NY, USA: Farrar, Strauss and Giroux.

Jacobsen, M-E. (1999). *The Gifted Adult: a Revolutionary Guide for Liberating Every-day Genius.* New York, NY, USA: Ballantine Books.

Judith, A. (1996, 2004). *Eastern Body, Western Mind: Psychology and the Chakra system as a path to the Self.* Berkeley, CA, USA: Celestial Arts.

Kempen, A. van (Ed.) (2006). *Reader Hoogbegaafd-en-Werk 2006 (Reader Gifted-at-Work 2006).* Zoetermeer, the Netherlands: Free Musketeers.

Keirsey, D. & Bates, M. (1978) *Please Understand Me: Character & temperament types.* Del Mar, CA, USA: Prometheus Nemesis Book Company.

Kerr, B. A. (1994). *Smart Girls (Revised Edition) - A New Psychology of Girls, Women, and Giftedness.* Scottsdale, AZ, USA: Great Potential Press, Inc.

Kerr, B. A., Cohn, S.J. (2001). *Smart Boys: Talent, Manhood, and the Search for Meaning.* Scottsdale, AZ, USA: Great Potential Press, Inc.

Kooijman-van Thiel, M. (Ed.) (2008). *Hoogbegaafd. Dat zie je zó! (Gifted. That is so obvious!)* Ede, The Netherlands: Oya Productions.

Kuipers, W. (2007). How to charm gifted adults into admitting giftedness, their own and somebody else's. *Advanced Development Journal 11,* 9-25. Denver, CO, USA: Inst. for the Study of Advanced Development.

Kuipers, W. (2007). *Verleid jezelf tot excellentie! Gereedschap voor extra intelligente mensen (Tempt yourself into excellence! Tools for extra intelligent people).* Zoetermeer, the Netherlands: Free Musketeers.

Lakoff, G., Johnson, M. (1999). *Philosophy in the Flesh: The embodied Mind and its Challenge to Western Thought.* New York, NY, USA: Basic Books.

Laney, M.O. (2002). *The Introvert Advantage: how to thrive in an extravert world.* New York NY, USA: Workman.

Moore, R.L. & Gillette, D. (1990). *King Warrior Magician Lover: Rediscovering the Archetypes of the Mature Masculine.* New York NY, USA: HarperCollins.

Nauta, N. & Ronner, S. (2007). *Ongeleide projectielen op koers: werken en leven met hoogbegaafdheid (Unguided missiles on course: working and living with giftedness).* Amsterdam, the Netherlands: Harcourt.

Piechowski, M.M. (2006) *"Mellow Out," They Say. If I Only Could. Intensities and Sensitivities of the Young and Bright.* Madison, WI, USA: Yunasa Books.

Powell, P. & Haden, T. (1984). The intellectual and psychosocial nature of extreme giftedness. *Roeper Review, 6(3) 131-133.*

Quinn, R.E. (1996). *Deep Change: Discovering the Leader Within.* San Francisco, CA, USA: Jossey-Bass.

Silverman, L.K. (1998). Personality and learning styles of gifted children. In J. VanTassel-Baska (Ed.), *Excellence in educating gifted and talented learners* (3rd ed.) (pp. 29-65). Denver, Co, USA: Love.

Silverman, L.K. (2002). *Upside-down Brilliance, the Visual-Spatial Learner.* Denver, Co, USA: DeLeon Publishing.

Silverman, L.K. (2006). I'm Not Gifted, I'm Just Busy. Gifted Adults: Unrecognized Giftedness in Women. In A. van Kempen (red.), *Reader Hoogbegaafd-en-Werk 2006.* Zoetermeer, the Netherlands: Free Musketeers.

Streznewski, M.K. (1999). *Gifted Grownups: the Mixed Blessings of Extraordinary Potential.* New York, NY, USA: John Wiley & Sons.

Thomas Jr., R. Roosevelt. "Diversity Management: An Essential Craft for Leaders" *Leader to Leader, 41* (Summer 2006): 45-49.

Tolan, S.S. (1999). Self-Knowledge, Self-Esteem and the Gifted Adult, *Advanced Development Journal (8) 147-150.*

Waal, F. de. (2009). *The Age of Empathy; Nature's Lessons for a Kinder Society.* New York, NY, USA: Harmony Books

Websites

A small collection of websites, a vast source of information. (as of fall 2010)

http://www.ximension.com
Website of Kuipers & Van Kempen. Information on this book and new developments, link to services.

http://www.gifteddevelopment.com
Website of the Gifted Development Center. Information on giftedness, the Advanced Development Journal and many articles and books.

http://www.visualspatial.org
The Visual-Spatial Resource. Extensive information on imaginal thinking.

http://highability.org
A member of the talentdevelop.com family, focusing on advanced development of gifted and talented adults.

http://www.hoagiesgifted.org/gifted_adults.htm
Extensive references on adult giftedness, brought together by Carolyn K.

http://www.sengifted.org/articles_index.shtml
The article database of SENG, Supporting Emotional Needs of the Gifted.

Index

A
archetypes, 62, 64, 75, 79, 88–92
autonomy, ix, 2, 14, 101, 107–9, 112, 116, 121, 142, 150, 159, 167

B
Baron-Cohen, Simon, 134
Berens, Linda, 73
Bly, Robert, 157
Boosten, Karien, 23

C
Cameron, Kim, 127
chakra, 123, 135, 136, 147, 148–53, 154, 156, 158, 159–66
complexity, xiii, 16, 35, 47, 48, 52, 54, 64, 90, 91, 99, 121, 134
Covey, Stephen, 4
creativity, 9, 26, 51, 55, 67, 83, 91, 152, 156, 163, 165

D
Dabrowski, Kazimierz, 83, 121
diversity, x, 7, 13, 32, 35, 44, 100, 101, 102, 143
diversity management, 51–54
drive, 5, 16, 35, 47, 48, 54, 64, 89, 91, 99, 117, 129
Dweck, Carol, 124–27, 141

E
effectiveness, x, xiv, 1, 3, 4, 7, 8, 13, 23, 53, 55, 57, 68, 74, 82, 99, 101, 104, 118, 122, 123, 130, 141, 142, 148, 156
embodied cognition, 123, 128–31, 134
empathy. *See also* extra empathy
Ensing-Wijn, Mechel, 68
excellence, 3, 6, 28, 55, 79, 88, 94, 101, 102–4, 107, 120–21, 131, 147, 156, 160
expression, xiii, 7, 10, 17, 21, 22, 26, 28, 35, 50, 57, 62, 66, 77, 84, 85, 88, 91, 93, 100, 103, 104, 105, 106, 113, 116, 118, 120, 132, 135, 147, 149, 152, 156, 159–66
extra empathy, 8, 62, 64, 79–82, 109, 119, 133, 144, 160
extra receptivity, 62, 64
extra task-orientation, 8, 62, 64, 79–82, 109, 119, 133, 144
extraversion, 62, 64, 75–76
extreme intelligence. *See also* Xi, extreme

G
Gardner, Howard, 2, 65
Geffen, Grethe van, 51
gift, 1, 5, 7, 13, 21, 25–28, 30, 61, 92, 107, 112–17, 166
giftedness, ix, 1, 4, 8, 20–25, 26, 35, 40, 42, 61, 78, 93, 115, 122, 135, 153, 180
gift-exchange, 26, 112, 113, 115, 117, 121

H
Hyde, Lewis, x, 26, 112, 113

I
Iacoboni, Marco, 123, 131
imaginal thinking, 17, 62, 64, 67–73, 78, 133
independent, 100, 104, 105, 107, 112, 116, 117, 123

intensity, 16, 17, 35, 47, 48, 54, 64, 81, 90, 91, 99, 108, 121, 129, 142, 148, 153
introversion, 62, 64, 75–76
introvert, 75–76, 82, 161
intuition, 16, 67, 75, 85
IQ score, 17, 20, 23–24, 26, 31, 67, 92, 126, 129, 130

J

Jacobsen, Mary-Elaine, 15, 47
Judith, Anodea, 135, 149, 158

K

Keirsey, David, 73
Kerr, Barbara, 118
Kooijman-van Thiel, Maud, 24

L

labyrinth, 123, 131, 135, 136, 147, 153–56, 157, 158, 159–66
Lakoff, George, 123, 128
Laney, Marti Olsen, 75
leadership, 20, 102, 104, 105, 122

M

market economy, 26, 107, 112–17
mastery, 6, 7, 8, 74, 101, 102, 104, 107, 117–20, 121, 124, 131, 147
mindset, 33, 124–27, 141, 143
mirror neurons, 54, 123, 128, 131–34
Moore, Robert, 88
multiple intelligences, 2, 26, 29, 62, 64, 65–66, 102, 129, 142

N

Nauta, Noks, 9, 35

O

Oberndorff-De Wilde, Ariane, 8

overexcitability, 83

P

perfectionism, 14, 17, 158
performance, 5, 6, 7, 21, 26, 30, 33, 40, 44, 51, 78, 84, 101, 104, 105, 106, 107, 115, 116, 117–20, 124, 131, 134, 141, 166
Piechowski, Michael, 83, 84
positive disintegration, theory of, 83, 121
Powell, Philip, 94
precision instrument, 61, 144, 149

Q

Quinn, Robert, 120

R

rapport, 101, 107–9, 112, 116, 122, 139

S

Silverman, Linda, ix–xi, 67, 75, 78
stagnation, 10, 17, 28, 82, 114, 116, 135, 138, 147, 149, 153, 156, 157–66
Streznewski, Marylou, 104
striver, 100, 104, 105, 107, 112, 115, 117
super pioneer, 116
superstar, 100, 104, 107, 112, 115, 116

T

task-orientation. *See also* extra task-orientation
temperament, 62, 64, 73–75, 100, 103
Thomas Jr., Roosevelt, 52
Tolan, Stephanie, 31

U

underperformance, 22

V

verbal thinking, 17, 62, 64, 67–73, 133

X

Xe. *See also* extra empathy
Xi, 2
   characteristics of, 39, 41, 57, 79, 107, 121, 141
   degree of, 29, 62, 92–95
   extreme, 92–95
Xidentity, 6, 41, 56, 61, 89, 100, 109, 129, 143

Ximension, 3, 7, 8, 13, 44, 45, 54–57, 72, 77, 79, 99, 109, 179
Ximension foundation, 179
Xinasty, 36, 56, 64, 77–79, 88, 95, 118, 144
Xr, 82–85, 107, 121, 130
   emotional, 83, 85, 129, 130
   imaginational, 85
   intellectual, 85
   psychomotor, 78, 84, 129
   sensual, 75, 84, 129, 130
Xt. *See also* extra task-orientation

Paul is intensely concentrating on his camera and the pictures that he has made. He becomes oblivious to what happens around him. His zeal for his craft stretches his borders regularly. Photograph by Mariska Mallee.

Photographs, paintings, and figures in the book

How can one bring extra intelligence into view?
Annelien van Kempen decided to ask artist/photographer Paul Rüpp (Amersfoort, 1958) to give his vision on this question through his photographs. The seven portraits of *Annelien, Georgina, Hans, Magda, Mariska, Paul* and *Willem* were made especially for this book.
For Paul, Xi covers many aspects. He always recognizes characteristics of Xi such as intellectually able in their domains, the need for autonomy and curiosity. He is also fascinated by the hands of his XIPs and the way their body language shows their intensity. He made the photographs in the XIP's personal or work environment, where he/she would feel at ease and be extra visible as an XIP.
The photographs can be found on page 18, 19, 110, 111, 145 and 146.
I want to thank Hans, Annelien, Magda, Mariska, Georgina and Paul for their generosity in allowing their photographs to be taken and to be included in this book. I also thank Paul for his craftsmanship and perseverance in preparing the photographs for inclusion in this book.

The two paintings, *Family tree* on page 37 and *Humanity: the God with Thousand Eyes* on page 43, are by Mariska Mallee (Voorburg, 1959). Both were already included in my first book. Mariska's intuitive style and both themes match wonderfully with this book, too.
Paul has taken the photographs of the two paintings by his wife, Mariska has taken Paul's portrait. Paul and Mariska are the owners of studio/gallery "KunstRaam" (ArtWindow) in Voorburg, the Netherlands.

The glass objects, *Chariot of the Sun-God* and the two Goddesses: *Lady of Anatolia* and *Artemis* have been designed by Annelien van Kempen (Ooltgensplaat, 1955). She has blown the Chariot of the Sun-God herself and has teamed up with master glassblower Richard Price to make the goddesses. She took both photographs of her work.

I have inserted the photographs and paintings at specific places in the book to offer an extra association and inspiration to the themes that are discussed in the adjacent chapters or sections. I added some of Paul's comments on the portraits with the same purpose.

The photograph of the pair of garden sprinklers (figure 6, page 70) has been edited by Georgina Kuipers (Voorburg, 1992). She also made the portrait of Kuipers & Van Kempen on page 180 and of me on the back cover.

All figures have been designed by me, Willem Kuipers (Scheveningen, 1952). I also made the photographs of figure 6.
The figures are illustrations to where they are placed.

The Ximension Foundation

The mission of the Ximension Foundation is to enhance and support knowledge development, research, dissemination of information and education on the subject of extra intelligence and the resulting excellent expression, in the Netherlands and elsewhere.

The Foundation intends to support:

- Actions for disseminating knowledge;
- Specific development projects, both theoretical and practice oriented.
- Education projects;
- Expenditures for travel to exchange information with foreign partners;

The Foundation has been established by Annelien van Kempen in 2009 as a non-profit organization.

The Ximension Foundation board consists of:

Mrs. H.J.A. (Heleen) Grootendorst, chair;
Mr. L.J.F. (Frank) Cornelissen, secretary;
Mr. G. (Geert) Ensing, treasurer.

Adviser to the board: Mrs. L.E.J.M.C. (Annelien) van Kempen.

For more information, please contact the secretary of the board:

Mr. Frank Cornelissen
c/o Buitenruststraat 32
2271 HB Voorburg
the Netherlands
e-mail: xi@ximension.org.

Kuipers & Van Kempen

Kuipers & Van Kempen is based on the professional cooperation of Willem Kuipers and Annelien van Kempen in career coaching and development of identity for extra intelligent adults. Willem and Annelien share their house now that their daughter Georgina has left to study at the university.
Georgina was the first of the three to uncover the issue of giftedness and the implications for her own life, around 1999 at primary school. Annelien and Willem followed to their own surprise.
From that time, they have been working on the development and application of tools and methods to help extra intelligent adults in entering a new phase in their professional and personal development.

Annelien graduated from Erasmus University Rotterdam as a Master of Laws, was a business lawyer in the glass industry, created a studio for artists to make their hand blown glass, and is now working with extra intelligent adults. Additionally she is a glass artist herself. Pictures of her work can be found at her own website www.annelienvankempen.nl.

Willem graduated from Delft University of Technology as a mathematical engineer, studied and practised management consultancy, and currently enjoys counselling on career choice and development of identity. He sings in a choir and designs and builds labyrinths. Pictures and articles on his labyrinth work can be found at his website www.willemlabyrint.nl.

Made in the USA
Monee, IL
24 May 2025